Management Staff Plan
Complete Self-Assessment Guide

The guidance in this Self-Assessment is based ~~on manag~~ best practices and standards in business process architecture, design and quality management. The guidance is also based on the professional judgment of the individual collaborators listed in the Acknowledgments.

Notice of rights

Table of Contents

About The Art of Service

The Art of Service, Business Process Architects since 2000, is dedicated to helping stakeholders achieve excellence.

Defining, designing, creating, and implementing a process to solve a stakeholders challenge or meet an objective is the most valuable role… In EVERY group, company, organization and department.

Unless you're talking a one-time, single-use project, there should be a process. Whether that process is managed and implemented by humans, AI, or a combination of the two, it needs to be designed by someone with a complex enough perspective to ask the right questions.

Someone capable of asking the right questions and step back and say, 'What are we really trying to accomplish here? And is there a different way to look at it?'

With The Art of Service's Standard Requirements Self-Assessments, we empower people who can do just that — whether their title is marketer, entrepreneur, manager, salesperson, consultant, Business Process Manager, executive assistant, IT Manager, CIO etc... —they are the people who rule the future. They are people who watch the process as it happens, and ask the right questions to make the process work better.

Contact us when you need any support with this Self-Assessment and any help with templates, blue-prints and examples of standard documents you might need:

http://theartofservice.com
service@theartofservice.com

Acknowledgments

This checklist was developed under the auspices of The Art of Service, chaired by Gerardus Blokdyk.

Representatives from several client companies participated in the preparation of this Self-Assessment.

In addition, we are thankful for the design and printing services provided.

Included Resources - how to access

Included with your purchase of the book is the Management Staff Plan Self-Assessment Spreadsheet Dashboard which contains all questions and Self-Assessment areas and auto-generates insights, graphs, and project RACI planning - all with examples to get you started right away.

How? Simply send an email to
access@theartofservice.com
with this books' title in the subject to get the Management Staff Plan Self Assessment Tool right away.

You will receive the following contents with New and Updated specific criteria:

• The latest quick edition of the book in PDF

• The latest complete edition of the book in PDF, which criteria correspond to the criteria in...

• The Self-Assessment Excel Dashboard, and...

• Example pre-filled Self-Assessment Excel Dashboard to get familiar with results generation

• In-depth specific Checklists covering the topic

• Project management checklists and templates to assist with implementation

INCLUDES LIFETIME SELF ASSESSMENT UPDATES

Every self assessment comes with Lifetime Updates and Lifetime Free Updated Books. Lifetime Updates is an industry-first feature which allows you to receive verified self assessment updates, ensuring you always have the most accurate information at your fingertips.

Get it now- you will be glad you did - do it now, before you forget.

Send an email to **access@theartofservice.com** with this books' title in the subject to get the Management Staff Plan Self Assessment Tool right away.

Your feedback is invaluable to us

If you recently bought this book, we would love to hear from you! You can do this by writing a review on amazon (or the online store where you purchased this book) about your last purchase! As part of our continual service improvement process, we love to hear real client experiences and feedback.

How does it work?

To post a review on Amazon, just log in to your account and click on the Create Your Own Review button (under Customer Reviews) of the relevant product page. You can find examples of product reviews in Amazon. If you purchased from another online store, simply follow their procedures.

What happens when I submit my review?

Once you have submitted your review, send us an email at review@theartofservice.com with the link to your review so we can properly thank you for your feedback.

Purpose of this Self-Assessment

This Self-Assessment has been developed to improve understanding of the requirements and elements of Management Staff Plan, based on best practices and standards in business process architecture, design and quality management.

It is designed to allow for a rapid Self-Assessment to determine how closely existing management practices and procedures correspond to the elements of the Self-Assessment.

The criteria of requirements and elements of Management Staff Plan have been rephrased in the format of a Self-Assessment questionnaire, with a seven-criterion scoring system, as explained in this document.

In this format, even with limited background knowledge of

Management Staff Plan, a manager can quickly review existing operations to determine how they measure up to the standards. This in turn can serve as the starting point of a 'gap analysis' to identify management tools or system elements that might usefully be implemented in the organization to help improve overall performance.

How to use the Self-Assessment

On the following pages are a series of questions to identify to what extent your Management Staff Plan initiative is complete in comparison to the requirements set in standards.

To facilitate answering the questions, there is a space in front of each question to enter a score on a scale of '1' to '5'.

1 Strongly Disagree

2 Disagree

3 Neutral

4 Agree

5 Strongly Agree

Read the question and rate it with the following in front of mind:

'In my belief, the answer to this question is clearly defined'.

There are two ways in which you can choose to interpret this statement;
1. how aware are you that the answer to the question is clearly defined
2. for more in-depth analysis you can choose to gather

evidence and confirm the answer to the question. This obviously will take more time, most Self-Assessment users opt for the first way to interpret the question and dig deeper later on based on the outcome of the overall Self-Assessment.

A score of '1' would mean that the answer is not clear at all, where a '5' would mean the answer is crystal clear and defined. Leave emtpy when the question is not applicable or you don't want to answer it, you can skip it without affecting your score. Write your score in the space provided.

After you have responded to all the appropriate statements in each section, compute your average score for that section, using the formula provided, and round to the nearest tenth. Then transfer to the corresponding spoke in the Management Staff Plan Scorecard on the second next page of the Self-Assessment.

Your completed Management Staff Plan Scorecard will give you a clear presentation of which Management Staff Plan areas need attention.

Management Staff Plan
Scorecard Example

Example of how the finalized Scorecard can look like:

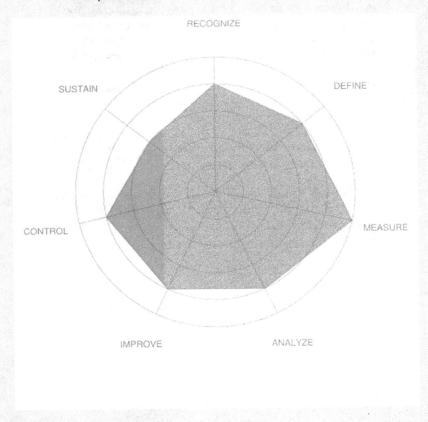

Management Staff Plan Scorecard

Your Scores:

BEGINNING OF THE SELF-ASSESSMENT:

CRITERION #1: RECOGNIZE

INTENT: Be aware of the need for change. Recognize that there is an unfavorable variation, problem or symptom.

In my belief, the answer to this question is clearly defined:

5 Strongly Agree

4 Agree

3 Neutral

2 Disagree

1 Strongly Disagree

1. What resources or support might you need?
<--- Score

2. Do you recognize management staff plan achievements?
<--- Score

3. What creative shifts do you need to take?
<--- Score

4. What are the minority interests and what amount of minority interests can be recognized?
<--- Score

5. How do you identify subcontractor relationships?
<--- Score

6. What else needs to be measured?
<--- Score

7. What prevents you from making the changes you know will make you a more effective management staff plan leader?
<--- Score

8. What does management staff plan success mean to the stakeholders?
<--- Score

9. What is the management staff plan problem definition? What do you need to resolve?
<--- Score

10. To what extent would your organization benefit from being recognized as a award recipient?
<--- Score

11. What do employees need in the short term?
<--- Score

12. What management staff plan coordination do you need?
<--- Score

13. Are you dealing with any of the same issues today

as yesterday? What can you do about this?
<--- Score

14. What would happen if management staff plan weren't done?
<--- Score

15. What problems are you facing and how do you consider management staff plan will circumvent those obstacles?
<--- Score

16. Why is this needed?
<--- Score

17. What should be considered when identifying available resources, constraints, and deadlines?
<--- Score

18. Is it clear when you think of the day ahead of you what activities and tasks you need to complete?
<--- Score

19. What are the clients issues and concerns?
<--- Score

20. Think about the people you identified for your management staff plan project and the project responsibilities you would assign to them, what kind of training do you think they would need to perform these responsibilities effectively?
<--- Score

21. What training and capacity building actions are needed to implement proposed reforms?
<--- Score

22. How do you take a forward-looking perspective in identifying management staff plan research related to market response and models?
<--- Score

23. Who needs to know?
<--- Score

24. For your management staff plan project, identify and describe the business environment, is there more than one layer to the business environment?
<--- Score

25. Do you need different information or graphics?
<--- Score

26. What extra resources will you need?
<--- Score

27. Are losses recognized in a timely manner?
<--- Score

28. Did you miss any major management staff plan issues?
<--- Score

29. Consider your own management staff plan project, what types of organizational problems do you think might be causing or affecting your problem, based on the work done so far?
<--- Score

30. Do you have/need 24-hour access to key personnel?
<--- Score

31. Who should resolve the management staff plan issues?
<--- Score

32. Is the need for organizational change recognized?
<--- Score

33. How are you going to measure success?
<--- Score

34. Would you recognize a threat from the inside?
<--- Score

35. Will a response program recognize when a crisis occurs and provide some level of response?
<--- Score

36. Does your organization need more management staff plan education?
<--- Score

37. Who defines the rules in relation to any given issue?
<--- Score

38. What information do users need?
<--- Score

39. How do you recognize an management staff plan objection?
<--- Score

40. Who are your key stakeholders who need to sign off?

<--- Score

41. When a management staff plan manager recognizes a problem, what options are available?
<--- Score

42. What are the management staff plan resources needed?
<--- Score

43. What is the recognized need?
<--- Score

44. How can auditing be a preventative security measure?
<--- Score

45. Are there any specific expectations or concerns about the management staff plan team, management staff plan itself?
<--- Score

46. Which information does the management staff plan business case need to include?
<--- Score

47. Does the problem have ethical dimensions?
<--- Score

48. How are training requirements identified?
<--- Score

49. What are the timeframes required to resolve each of the issues/problems?
<--- Score

50. Which needs are not included or involved?
<--- Score

51. Are problem definition and motivation clearly presented?
<--- Score

52. What are the stakeholder objectives to be achieved with management staff plan?
<--- Score

53. Are employees recognized or rewarded for performance that demonstrates the highest levels of integrity?
<--- Score

54. Where do you need to exercise leadership?
<--- Score

55. What is the extent or complexity of the management staff plan problem?
<--- Score

56. Are there any revenue recognition issues?
<--- Score

57. How does it fit into your organizational needs and tasks?
<--- Score

58. Is it needed?
<--- Score

59. What is the problem or issue?
<--- Score

60. How much are sponsors, customers, partners, stakeholders involved in management staff plan? In other words, what are the risks, if management staff plan does not deliver successfully?
<--- Score

61. What activities does the governance board need to consider?
<--- Score

62. Can management personnel recognize the monetary benefit of management staff plan?
<--- Score

63. What is the problem and/or vulnerability?
<--- Score

64. What do you need to start doing?
<--- Score

65. Whom do you really need or want to serve?
<--- Score

66. What are your needs in relation to management staff plan skills, labor, equipment, and markets?
<--- Score

67. What is the smallest subset of the problem you can usefully solve?
<--- Score

68. Who needs to know about management staff plan?
<--- Score

69. Do you need to avoid or amend any

management staff plan activities?
<--- Score

70. How do you recognize an objection?
<--- Score

71. Are there management staff plan problems defined?
<--- Score

72. Who else hopes to benefit from it?
<--- Score

73. To what extent does each concerned units management team recognize management staff plan as an effective investment?
<--- Score

74. Looking at each person individually – does every one have the qualities which are needed to work in this group?
<--- Score

75. How are the management staff plan's objectives aligned to the group's overall stakeholder strategy?
<--- Score

76. What needs to stay?
<--- Score

77. What tools and technologies are needed for a custom management staff plan project?
<--- Score

78. What management staff plan events should you attend?

<--- Score

79. How many trainings, in total, are needed?
<--- Score

80. Are your goals realistic? Do you need to redefine your problem? Perhaps the problem has changed or maybe you have reached your goal and need to set a new one?
<--- Score

81. Which issues are too important to ignore?
<--- Score

82. Who needs budgets?
<--- Score

83. Will it solve real problems?
<--- Score

84. Where is training needed?
<--- Score

85. Why the need?
<--- Score

86. What vendors make products that address the management staff plan needs?
<--- Score

87. What management staff plan capabilities do you need?
<--- Score

88. As a sponsor, customer or management, how important is it to meet goals, objectives?

<--- Score

89. Are employees recognized for desired behaviors?
<--- Score

90. What situation(s) led to this management staff
plan Self Assessment?
<--- Score

91. Are there regulatory / compliance issues?
<--- Score

92. Is the quality assurance team identified?
<--- Score

93. What are the expected benefits of management
staff plan to the stakeholder?
<--- Score

Add up total points for this section:
_____ = Total points for this section

Divided by: _____ (number of
statements answered) = _____
Average score for this section

Transfer your score to the management
staff plan Index at the beginning of the
Self-Assessment.

CRITERION #2: DEFINE:

INTENT: Formulate the stakeholder problem. Define the problem, needs and objectives.

In my belief, the answer to this question is clearly defined:

5 Strongly Agree

4 Agree

3 Neutral

2 Disagree

1 Strongly Disagree

1. How would you define the culture at your organization, how susceptible is it to management staff plan changes?
<--- Score

2. Is there a completed, verified, and validated high-level 'as is' (not 'should be' or 'could be') stakeholder process map?
<--- Score

3. If substitutes have been appointed, have they been briefed on the management staff plan goals and received regular communications as to the progress to date?
<--- Score

4. How often are the team meetings?
<--- Score

5. Has the direction changed at all during the course of management staff plan? If so, when did it change and why?
<--- Score

6. Has the management staff plan work been fairly and/or equitably divided and delegated among team members who are qualified and capable to perform the work? Has everyone contributed?
<--- Score

7. What would be the goal or target for a management staff plan's improvement team?
<--- Score

8. How do you hand over management staff plan context?
<--- Score

9. How do you keep key subject matter experts in the loop?
<--- Score

10. How do you build the right business case?
<--- Score

11. What are the rough order estimates on cost savings/opportunities that management staff plan brings?
<--- Score

12. Where can you gather more information?
<--- Score

13. Who approved the management staff plan scope?
<--- Score

14. How will variation in the actual durations of each activity be dealt with to ensure that the expected management staff plan results are met?
<--- Score

15. In what way can you redefine the criteria of choice clients have in your category in your favor?
<--- Score

16. How would you define management staff plan leadership?
<--- Score

17. The political context: who holds power?
<--- Score

18. How have you defined all management staff plan requirements first?
<--- Score

19. Has a team charter been developed and communicated?
<--- Score

20. Will a management staff plan production

readiness review be required?
<--- Score

21. Is there any additional management staff plan definition of success?
<--- Score

22. How do you gather the stories?
<--- Score

23. What is the scope of the management staff plan work?
<--- Score

24. Is management staff plan currently on schedule according to the plan?
<--- Score

25. How does the management staff plan manager ensure against scope creep?
<--- Score

26. Are customer(s) identified and segmented according to their different needs and requirements?
<--- Score

27. Have specific policy objectives been defined?
<--- Score

28. Who are the management staff plan improvement team members, including Management Leads and Coaches?
<--- Score

29. When are meeting minutes sent out? Who is on the distribution list?

<--- Score

30. What is a worst-case scenario for losses?
<--- Score

31. Is special management staff plan user knowledge required?
<--- Score

32. How will the management staff plan team and the group measure complete success of management staff plan?
<--- Score

33. Why are you doing management staff plan and what is the scope?
<--- Score

34. How did the management staff plan manager receive input to the development of a management staff plan improvement plan and the estimated completion dates/times of each activity?
<--- Score

35. What information should you gather?
<--- Score

36. What critical content must be communicated – who, what, when, where, and how?
<--- Score

37. What defines best in class?
<--- Score

38. What sources do you use to gather information for a management staff plan study?

<--- Score

39. What is the worst case scenario?
<--- Score

40. Is the management staff plan scope manageable?
<--- Score

41. What are the boundaries of the scope? What is in bounds and what is not? What is the start point? What is the stop point?
<--- Score

42. Is the management staff plan scope complete and appropriately sized?
<--- Score

43. How do you manage unclear management staff plan requirements?
<--- Score

44. What constraints exist that might impact the team?
<--- Score

45. Does the team have regular meetings?
<--- Score

46. Is the team adequately staffed with the desired cross-functionality? If not, what additional resources are available to the team?
<--- Score

47. Has a project plan, Gantt chart, or similar been developed/completed?
<--- Score

48. Do you all define management staff plan in the same way?
<--- Score

49. Are the management staff plan requirements testable?
<--- Score

50. Do the problem and goal statements meet the SMART criteria (specific, measurable, attainable, relevant, and time-bound)?
<--- Score

51. What management staff plan services do you require?
<--- Score

52. Is it clearly defined in and to your organization what you do?
<--- Score

53. What customer feedback methods were used to solicit their input?
<--- Score

54. Do you have organizational privacy requirements?
<--- Score

55. What are the core elements of the management staff plan business case?
<--- Score

56. What is the scope of the management staff plan effort?

<--- Score

57. Do you have a management staff plan success story or case study ready to tell and share?
<--- Score

58. Are required metrics defined, what are they?
<--- Score

59. How do you gather management staff plan requirements?
<--- Score

60. Are task requirements clearly defined?
<--- Score

61. What specifically is the problem? Where does it occur? When does it occur? What is its extent?
<--- Score

62. Is scope creep really all bad news?
<--- Score

63. Is the scope of management staff plan defined?
<--- Score

64. What are the tasks and definitions?
<--- Score

65. What sort of initial information to gather?
<--- Score

66. When is/was the management staff plan start date?
<--- Score

67. What is the context?
<--- Score

68. Is the work to date meeting requirements?
<--- Score

69. Has a high-level 'as is' process map been completed, verified and validated?
<--- Score

70. What knowledge or experience is required?
<--- Score

71. What is the definition of success?
<--- Score

72. Will team members perform management staff plan work when assigned and in a timely fashion?
<--- Score

73. How do you gather requirements?
<--- Score

74. Is there a completed SIPOC representation, describing the Suppliers, Inputs, Process, Outputs, and Customers?
<--- Score

75. Are resources adequate for the scope?
<--- Score

76. Are improvement team members fully trained on management staff plan?
<--- Score

77. When is the estimated completion date?

<--- Score

78. How do you catch management staff plan definition inconsistencies?
<--- Score

79. What are (control) requirements for management staff plan Information?
<--- Score

80. Have all of the relationships been defined properly?
<--- Score

81. How is the team tracking and documenting its work?
<--- Score

82. What baselines are required to be defined and managed?
<--- Score

83. Have all basic functions of management staff plan been defined?
<--- Score

84. Is there a clear management staff plan case definition?
<--- Score

85. What is the scope of management staff plan?
<--- Score

86. Scope of sensitive information?
<--- Score

87. Has your scope been defined?

<--- Score

88. Is management staff plan required?

<--- Score

89. What are the record-keeping requirements of management staff plan activities?

<--- Score

90. What system do you use for gathering management staff plan information?

<--- Score

91. Has/have the customer(s) been identified?

<--- Score

92. What information do you gather?

<--- Score

93. Has everyone on the team, including the team leaders, been properly trained?

<--- Score

94. Who defines (or who defined) the rules and roles?

<--- Score

95. What are the compelling stakeholder reasons for embarking on management staff plan?

<--- Score

96. What scope to assess?

<--- Score

97. Has anyone else (internal or external to the group) attempted to solve this problem or a similar one

before? If so, what knowledge can be leveraged from these previous efforts?
<--- Score

98. Is management staff plan linked to key stakeholder goals and objectives?
<--- Score

99. Will team members regularly document their management staff plan work?
<--- Score

100. What is in the scope and what is not in scope?
<--- Score

101. What key stakeholder process output measure(s) does management staff plan leverage and how?
<--- Score

102. Are all requirements met?
<--- Score

103. Is the team formed and are team leaders (Coaches and Management Leads) assigned?
<--- Score

104. Are the management staff plan requirements complete?
<--- Score

105. Has the improvement team collected the 'voice of the customer' (obtained feedback – qualitative and quantitative)?
<--- Score

106. Is the improvement team aware of the different

versions of a process: what they think it is vs. what it actually is vs. what it should be vs. what it could be?
<--- Score

107. Is there a critical path to deliver management staff plan results?
<--- Score

108. What happens if management staff plan's scope changes?
<--- Score

109. What are the requirements for audit information?
<--- Score

110. Who is gathering information?
<--- Score

111. Is there a management staff plan management charter, including stakeholder case, problem and goal statements, scope, milestones, roles and responsibilities, communication plan?
<--- Score

112. Is data collected and displayed to better understand customer(s) critical needs and requirements.
<--- Score

113. How do you manage scope?
<--- Score

114. How are consistent management staff plan definitions important?
<--- Score

115. Is the team equipped with available and reliable resources?
<--- Score

116. Are there different segments of customers?
<--- Score

117. Are there any constraints known that bear on the ability to perform management staff plan work? How is the team addressing them?
<--- Score

118. What are the management staff plan tasks and definitions?
<--- Score

119. Is there regularly 100% attendance at the team meetings? If not, have appointed substitutes attended to preserve cross-functionality and full representation?
<--- Score

120. What are the Roles and Responsibilities for each team member and its leadership? Where is this documented?
<--- Score

121. Are approval levels defined for contracts and supplements to contracts?
<--- Score

122. Have the customer needs been translated into specific, measurable requirements? How?
<--- Score

123. How do you manage changes in management

staff plan requirements?
<--- Score

124. Are different versions of process maps needed to account for the different types of inputs?
<--- Score

125. Is full participation by members in regularly held team meetings guaranteed?
<--- Score

126. How can the value of management staff plan be defined?
<--- Score

127. What gets examined?
<--- Score

128. Is the current 'as is' process being followed? If not, what are the discrepancies?
<--- Score

129. How was the 'as is' process map developed, reviewed, verified and validated?
<--- Score

130. Are roles and responsibilities formally defined?
<--- Score

131. Has a management staff plan requirement not been met?
<--- Score

132. Who is gathering management staff plan information?
<--- Score

133. What are the dynamics of the communication plan?
<--- Score

134. What was the context?
<--- Score

135. Are accountability and ownership for management staff plan clearly defined?
<--- Score

136. What intelligence can you gather?
<--- Score

137. What management staff plan requirements should be gathered?
<--- Score

138. What are the management staff plan use cases?
<--- Score

139. What is the definition of management staff plan excellence?
<--- Score

Add up total points for this section:
_ _ _ _ _ = Total points for this section

Divided by: _ _ _ _ _ _ (number of statements answered) = _ _ _ _ _ _
Average score for this section

Transfer your score to the management staff plan Index at the beginning of the

Self-Assessment.

CRITERION #3: MEASURE:

INTENT: Gather the correct data.
Measure the current performance and
evolution of the situation.

In my belief, the answer to this
question is clearly defined:

5 Strongly Agree

4 Agree

3 Neutral

2 Disagree

1 Strongly Disagree

1. How frequently do you verify your management staff plan strategy?
<--- Score

2. What is the root cause(s) of the problem?
<--- Score

3. What is your decision requirements diagram?
<--- Score

4. What details are required of the management staff plan cost structure?
<--- Score

5. How do you verify the management staff plan requirements quality?
<--- Score

6. What causes mismanagement?
<--- Score

7. Why do you expend time and effort to implement measurement, for whom?
<--- Score

8. Do you have an issue in getting priority?
<--- Score

9. How do you quantify and qualify impacts?
<--- Score

10. How do your measurements capture actionable management staff plan information for use in exceeding your customers expectations and securing your customers engagement?
<--- Score

11. How do you verify and develop ideas and innovations?
<--- Score

12. How will you measure success?
<--- Score

13. Do you verify that corrective actions were taken?

<--- Score

14. How long to keep data and how to manage retention costs?
<--- Score

15. What is the total fixed cost?
<--- Score

16. What disadvantage does this cause for the user?
<--- Score

17. What are the management staff plan investment costs?
<--- Score

18. How will measures be used to manage and adapt?
<--- Score

19. Are missed management staff plan opportunities costing your organization money?
<--- Score

20. What are your operating costs?
<--- Score

21. How do you measure variability?
<--- Score

22. What are the costs of delaying management staff plan action?
<--- Score

23. What are your customers expectations and measures?

<--- Score

24. What do people want to verify?
<--- Score

25. Is it possible to estimate the impact of unanticipated complexity such as wrong or failed assumptions, feedback, etcetera on proposed reforms?
<--- Score

26. Do you have any cost management staff plan limitation requirements?
<--- Score

27. How is progress measured?
<--- Score

28. What are hidden management staff plan quality costs?
<--- Score

29. How are measurements made?
<--- Score

30. Is the solution cost-effective?
<--- Score

31. What would it cost to replace your technology?
<--- Score

32. What are your primary costs, revenues, assets?
<--- Score

33. How do you measure lifecycle phases?
<--- Score

34. How do you verify your resources?
<--- Score

35. What drives O&M cost?
<--- Score

36. What is the cause of any management staff plan gaps?
<--- Score

37. Where is it measured?
<--- Score

38. What are the estimated costs of proposed changes?
<--- Score

39. What does verifying compliance entail?
<--- Score

40. What are the management staff plan key cost drivers?
<--- Score

41. What are the costs?
<--- Score

42. What does your operating model cost?
<--- Score

43. What methods are feasible and acceptable to estimate the impact of reforms?
<--- Score

44. How do you verify management staff plan

completeness and accuracy?
<--- Score

45. Who pays the cost?
<--- Score

46. What does losing customers cost your organization?
<--- Score

47. How can you manage cost down?
<--- Score

48. What is measured? Why?
<--- Score

49. Did you tackle the cause or the symptom?
<--- Score

50. What would be a real cause for concern?
<--- Score

51. Does the management staff plan task fit the client's priorities?
<--- Score

52. How can you measure management staff plan in a systematic way?
<--- Score

53. How do you prevent mis-estimating cost?
<--- Score

54. How can you reduce costs?
<--- Score

55. Are there measurements based on task performance?

<--- Score

56. What happens if cost savings do not materialize?

<--- Score

57. What could cause you to change course?

<--- Score

58. How can you reduce the costs of obtaining inputs?

<--- Score

59. Is there an opportunity to verify requirements?

<--- Score

60. When should you bother with diagrams?

<--- Score

61. Is the cost worth the management staff plan effort ?

<--- Score

62. What measurements are possible, practicable and meaningful?

<--- Score

63. What is an unallowable cost?

<--- Score

64. Does management have the right priorities among projects?

<--- Score

65. What is your management staff plan quality

cost segregation study?

<--- Score

66. Do you aggressively reward and promote the people who have the biggest impact on creating excellent management staff plan services/ products?

<--- Score

67. What tests verify requirements?

<--- Score

68. Are you aware of what could cause a problem?

<--- Score

69. How frequently do you track management staff plan measures?

<--- Score

70. How can a management staff plan test verify your ideas or assumptions?

<--- Score

71. How will costs be allocated?

<--- Score

72. What are the costs and benefits?

<--- Score

73. Are management staff plan vulnerabilities categorized and prioritized?

<--- Score

74. Who is involved in verifying compliance?

<--- Score

75. What is the management staff plan business impact?
<--- Score

76. Do you effectively measure and reward individual and team performance?
<--- Score

77. How will your organization measure success?
<--- Score

78. Are you able to realize any cost savings?
<--- Score

79. Are the management staff plan benefits worth its costs?
<--- Score

80. Which costs should be taken into account?
<--- Score

81. Have you made assumptions about the shape of the future, particularly its impact on your customers and competitors?
<--- Score

82. How are you verifying it?
<--- Score

83. What are the uncertainties surrounding estimates of impact?
<--- Score

84. How do you control the overall costs of your work processes?
<--- Score

85. What do you measure and why?
<--- Score

86. Are there competing management staff plan priorities?
<--- Score

87. What are your key management staff plan organizational performance measures, including key short and longer-term financial measures?
<--- Score

88. Has a cost center been established?
<--- Score

89. What evidence is there and what is measured?
<--- Score

90. What causes innovation to fail or succeed in your organization?
<--- Score

91. How do you verify the authenticity of the data and information used?
<--- Score

92. Are actual costs in line with budgeted costs?
<--- Score

93. Does a management staff plan quantification method exist?
<--- Score

94. What is the total cost related to deploying management staff plan, including any consulting or

professional services?

<--- Score

95. How is performance measured?

<--- Score

96. What causes extra work or rework?

<--- Score

97. What relevant entities could be measured?

<--- Score

98. Are there any easy-to-implement alternatives to management staff plan? Sometimes other solutions are available that do not require the cost implications of a full-blown project?

<--- Score

99. Are you taking your company in the direction of better and revenue or cheaper and cost?

<--- Score

100. What could cause delays in the schedule?

<--- Score

101. Have design-to-cost goals been established?

<--- Score

102. What are the types and number of measures to use?

<--- Score

103. How will success or failure be measured?

<--- Score

104. Are indirect costs charged to the management

staff plan program?

<--- Score

105. How will you measure your management staff plan effectiveness?

<--- Score

106. How can you measure the performance?

<--- Score

107. How much does it cost?

<--- Score

108. Will management staff plan have an impact on current business continuity, disaster recovery processes and/or infrastructure?

<--- Score

109. Do the benefits outweigh the costs?

<--- Score

110. Are the measurements objective?

<--- Score

111. At what cost?

<--- Score

112. What are you verifying?

<--- Score

113. What can be used to verify compliance?

<--- Score

114. How are costs allocated?

<--- Score

115. What potential environmental factors impact the management staff plan effort?
<--- Score

116. What are allowable costs?
<--- Score

117. What are the strategic priorities for this year?
<--- Score

118. Where is the cost?
<--- Score

119. What are the operational costs after management staff plan deployment?
<--- Score

120. How do you measure efficient delivery of management staff plan services?
<--- Score

121. What measurements are being captured?
<--- Score

122. How do you measure success?
<--- Score

123. How will effects be measured?
<--- Score

124. What does a Test Case verify?
<--- Score

125. What causes investor action?
<--- Score

126. How is the value delivered by management staff plan being measured?
<--- Score

127. When a disaster occurs, who gets priority?
<--- Score

128. Are the units of measure consistent?
<--- Score

129. When are costs are incurred?
<--- Score

130. What harm might be caused?
<--- Score

131. How do you verify performance?
<--- Score

132. How do you aggregate measures across priorities?
<--- Score

133. Do you have a flow diagram of what happens?
<--- Score

134. What is the cost of rework?
<--- Score

135. Who should receive measurement reports?
<--- Score

136. What are the current costs of the management staff plan process?
<--- Score

137. How do you verify if management staff plan is built right?
<--- Score

138. The approach of traditional management staff plan works for detail complexity but is focused on a systematic approach rather than an understanding of the nature of systems themselves, what approach will permit your organization to deal with the kind of unpredictable emergent behaviors that dynamic complexity can introduce?
<--- Score

139. What users will be impacted?
<--- Score

140. Which management staff plan impacts are significant?
<--- Score

141. How to cause the change?
<--- Score

142. How do you verify and validate the management staff plan data?
<--- Score

Add up total points for this section:
_ _ _ _ _ = Total points for this section

Divided by: _ _ _ _ _ _ (number of statements answered) = _ _ _ _ _ _
Average score for this section

Transfer your score to the management staff plan Index at the beginning of the

Self-Assessment.

CRITERION #4: ANALYZE:

1. How can risk management be tied procedurally to process elements?
<--- Score

2. What does the data say about the performance of the stakeholder process?
<--- Score

3. Were there any improvement opportunities identified from the process analysis?

<--- Score

4. Is there a strict change management process?
<--- Score

5. Are all staff in core management staff plan subjects Highly Qualified?
<--- Score

6. What management staff plan metrics are outputs of the process?
<--- Score

7. Where can you get qualified talent today?
<--- Score

8. What quality tools were used to get through the analyze phase?
<--- Score

9. What qualifications do management staff plan leaders need?
<--- Score

10. What management staff plan data do you gather or use now?
<--- Score

11. What do you need to qualify?
<--- Score

12. What qualifications are necessary?
<--- Score

13. Do you, as a leader, bounce back quickly from setbacks?

<--- Score

14. What were the financial benefits resulting from any 'ground fruit or low-hanging fruit' (quick fixes)?
<--- Score

15. Do several people in different organizational units assist with the management staff plan process?
<--- Score

16. What process improvements will be needed?
<--- Score

17. What are the management staff plan business drivers?
<--- Score

18. Who gets your output?
<--- Score

19. Do you understand your management processes today?
<--- Score

20. How is the management staff plan Value Stream Mapping managed?
<--- Score

21. What are the disruptive management staff plan technologies that enable your organization to radically change your business processes?
<--- Score

22. How will the management staff plan data be captured?
<--- Score

23. How do you use management staff plan data and information to support organizational decision making and innovation?
<--- Score

24. Who owns what data?
<--- Score

25. How much data can be collected in the given timeframe?
<--- Score

26. What is the management staff plan Driver?
<--- Score

27. How do you ensure that the management staff plan opportunity is realistic?
<--- Score

28. Have you defined which data is gathered how?
<--- Score

29. Think about some of the processes you undertake within your organization, which do you own?
<--- Score

30. Is the final output clearly identified?
<--- Score

31. Is the performance gap determined?
<--- Score

32. How do you identify specific management staff plan investment opportunities and emerging trends?
<--- Score

33. What other jobs or tasks affect the performance of the steps in the management staff plan process?
<--- Score

34. What are your management staff plan processes?
<--- Score

35. Is the suppliers process defined and controlled?
<--- Score

36. How do you measure the operational performance of your key work systems and processes, including productivity, cycle time, and other appropriate measures of process effectiveness, efficiency, and innovation?
<--- Score

37. Is there an established change management process?
<--- Score

38. How is the way you as the leader think and process information affecting your organizational culture?
<--- Score

39. What qualifies as competition?
<--- Score

40. What are the management staff plan design outputs?
<--- Score

41. What process should you select for improvement?
<--- Score

42. Has data output been validated?
<--- Score

43. Who is involved with workflow mapping?
<--- Score

44. What are your key performance measures or indicators and in-process measures for the control and improvement of your management staff plan processes?
<--- Score

45. What are your outputs?
<--- Score

46. How difficult is it to qualify what management staff plan ROI is?
<--- Score

47. How do mission and objectives affect the management staff plan processes of your organization?
<--- Score

48. Where is the data coming from to measure compliance?
<--- Score

49. What tools were used to narrow the list of possible causes?
<--- Score

50. Are your outputs consistent?
<--- Score

51. Is data and process analysis, root cause analysis

and quantifying the gap/opportunity in place?
<--- Score

52. Do staff qualifications match your project?
<--- Score

53. What output to create?
<--- Score

54. How is management staff plan data gathered?
<--- Score

55. Think about the functions involved in your management staff plan project, what processes flow from these functions?
<--- Score

56. Who qualifies to gain access to data?
<--- Score

57. How do you promote understanding that opportunity for improvement is not criticism of the status quo, or the people who created the status quo?
<--- Score

58. What will drive management staff plan change?
<--- Score

59. What data is gathered?
<--- Score

60. An organizationally feasible system request is one that considers the mission, goals and objectives of the organization, key questions are: is the management staff plan solution request practical and will it solve a problem or take advantage of an opportunity to

achieve company goals?
<--- Score

61. What are your current levels and trends in key management staff plan measures or indicators of product and process performance that are important to and directly serve your customers?
<--- Score

62. Did any additional data need to be collected?
<--- Score

63. Do quality systems drive continuous improvement?
<--- Score

64. What qualifications are needed?
<--- Score

65. What is the cost of poor quality as supported by the team's analysis?
<--- Score

66. Is pre-qualification of suppliers carried out?
<--- Score

67. What is the oversight process?
<--- Score

68. What resources go in to get the desired output?
<--- Score

69. Was a detailed process map created to amplify critical steps of the 'as is' stakeholder process?
<--- Score

70. What management staff plan data should be managed?
<--- Score

71. When should a process be art not science?
<--- Score

72. What are evaluation criteria for the output?
<--- Score

73. What data do you need to collect?
<--- Score

74. Was a cause-and-effect diagram used to explore the different types of causes (or sources of variation)?
<--- Score

75. What controls do you have in place to protect data?
<--- Score

76. Were Pareto charts (or similar) used to portray the 'heavy hitters' (or key sources of variation)?
<--- Score

77. How often will data be collected for measures?
<--- Score

78. What internal processes need improvement?
<--- Score

79. What are your current levels and trends in key measures or indicators of management staff plan product and process performance that are important to and directly serve your customers? How do these results compare with

the performance of your competitors and other organizations with similar offerings?
<--- Score

80. Record-keeping requirements flow from the records needed as inputs, outputs, controls and for transformation of a management staff plan process, are the records needed as inputs to the management staff plan process available?
<--- Score

81. Can you add value to the current management staff plan decision-making process (largely qualitative) by incorporating uncertainty modeling (more quantitative)?
<--- Score

82. Do your leaders quickly bounce back from setbacks?
<--- Score

83. What training and qualifications will you need?
<--- Score

84. Are you missing management staff plan opportunities?
<--- Score

85. How is data used for program management and improvement?
<--- Score

86. How do you implement and manage your work processes to ensure that they meet design requirements?
<--- Score

87. What management staff plan data should be collected?
<--- Score

88. How will the change process be managed?
<--- Score

89. Should you invest in industry-recognized qualifications?
<--- Score

90. What conclusions were drawn from the team's data collection and analysis? How did the team reach these conclusions?
<--- Score

91. Is the management staff plan process severely broken such that a re-design is necessary?
<--- Score

92. Do your contracts/agreements contain data security obligations?
<--- Score

93. Identify an operational issue in your organization, for example, could a particular task be done more quickly or more efficiently by management staff plan?
<--- Score

94. What successful thing are you doing today that may be blinding you to new growth opportunities?
<--- Score

95. What are the processes for audit reporting and

management?
<--- Score

96. Are management staff plan changes recognized early enough to be approved through the regular process?
<--- Score

97. Which management staff plan data should be retained?
<--- Score

98. How do you define collaboration and team output?
<--- Score

99. What are the necessary qualifications?
<--- Score

100. Is the gap/opportunity displayed and communicated in financial terms?
<--- Score

101. What did the team gain from developing a sub-process map?
<--- Score

102. How is the data gathered?
<--- Score

103. Were any designed experiments used to generate additional insight into the data analysis?
<--- Score

104. Who will facilitate the team and process?
<--- Score

105. Have the problem and goal statements been updated to reflect the additional knowledge gained from the analyze phase?
<--- Score

106. Where is management staff plan data gathered?
<--- Score

107. How many input/output points does it require?
<--- Score

108. What qualifications and skills do you need?
<--- Score

109. Has an output goal been set?
<--- Score

110. What tools were used to generate the list of possible causes?
<--- Score

111. Have any additional benefits been identified that will result from closing all or most of the gaps?
<--- Score

112. Did any value-added analysis or 'lean thinking' take place to identify some of the gaps shown on the 'as is' process map?
<--- Score

113. What were the crucial 'moments of truth' on the process map?
<--- Score

114. Are gaps between current performance and the

goal performance identified?
<--- Score

115. What is your organizations system for selecting qualified vendors?
<--- Score

116. What are your best practices for minimizing management staff plan project risk, while demonstrating incremental value and quick wins throughout the management staff plan project lifecycle?
<--- Score

117. What are the best opportunities for value improvement?
<--- Score

118. Is the required management staff plan data gathered?
<--- Score

119. How do your work systems and key work processes relate to and capitalize on your core competencies?
<--- Score

120. What management staff plan data will be collected?
<--- Score

121. How does the organization define, manage, and improve its management staff plan processes?
<--- Score

122. What is the output?

<--- Score

123. Do your employees have the opportunity to do what they do best everyday?
<--- Score

124. How has the management staff plan data been gathered?
<--- Score

125. What are the revised rough estimates of the financial savings/opportunity for management staff plan improvements?
<--- Score

126. What is your organizations process which leads to recognition of value generation?
<--- Score

127. What is the Value Stream Mapping?
<--- Score

128. How was the detailed process map generated, verified, and validated?
<--- Score

129. What is the complexity of the output produced?
<--- Score

130. What, related to, management staff plan processes does your organization outsource?
<--- Score

131. How are outputs preserved and protected?
<--- Score

132. What information qualified as important?

<--- Score

133. What types of data do your management staff plan indicators require?

<--- Score

134. What are the personnel training and qualifications required?

<--- Score

Add up total points for this section:
_ _ _ _ _ = Total points for this section

Divided by: _ _ _ _ _ _ (number of statements answered) = _ _ _ _ _ _
Average score for this section

Transfer your score to the management staff plan Index at the beginning of the Self-Assessment.

CRITERION #5: IMPROVE:

INTENT: Develop a practical solution. Innovate, establish and test the solution and to measure the results.

In my belief, the answer to this question is clearly defined:

5 Strongly Agree

4 Agree

3 Neutral

2 Disagree

1 Strongly Disagree

1. Risk factors: what are the characteristics of management staff plan that make it risky?
<--- Score

2. What criteria will you use to assess your management staff plan risks?
<--- Score

3. Explorations of the frontiers of management

staff plan will help you build influence, improve management staff plan, optimize decision making, and sustain change, what is your approach?
<--- Score

4. Are you assessing management staff plan and risk?
<--- Score

5. Do you combine technical expertise with business knowledge and management staff plan Key topics include lifecycles, development approaches, requirements and how to make a business case?
<--- Score

6. Are events managed to resolution?
<--- Score

7. What alternative responses are available to manage risk?
<--- Score

8. Would you develop a management staff plan Communication Strategy?
<--- Score

9. Have you achieved management staff plan improvements?
<--- Score

10. How are management staff plan risks managed?
<--- Score

11. How do you improve productivity?
<--- Score

12. What lessons, if any, from a pilot were incorporated into the design of the full-scale solution?
<--- Score

13. Who makes the management staff plan decisions in your organization?
<--- Score

14. How do you manage management staff plan risk?
<--- Score

15. When you map the key players in your own work and the types/domains of relationships with them, which relationships do you find easy and which challenging, and why?
<--- Score

16. How do you improve your likelihood of success ?
<--- Score

17. Who controls the risk?
<--- Score

18. Is the management staff plan solution sustainable?
<--- Score

19. How are policy decisions made and where?
<--- Score

20. How can the phases of management staff plan development be identified?
<--- Score

21. Will the controls trigger any other risks?
<--- Score

22. To what extent does management recognize management staff plan as a tool to increase the results?
<--- Score

23. Do vendor agreements bring new compliance risk ?
<--- Score

24. Who will be using the results of the measurement activities?
<--- Score

25. How will you measure the results?
<--- Score

26. Can you integrate quality management and risk management?
<--- Score

27. What were the underlying assumptions on the cost-benefit analysis?
<--- Score

28. Do those selected for the management staff plan team have a good general understanding of what management staff plan is all about?
<--- Score

29. What should a proof of concept or pilot accomplish?
<--- Score

30. Who manages management staff plan risk?
<--- Score

31. How can you improve management staff plan?
<--- Score

32. Do you have the optimal project management team structure?
<--- Score

33. What to do with the results or outcomes of measurements?
<--- Score

34. Was a management staff plan charter developed?
<--- Score

35. How do you deal with management staff plan risk?
<--- Score

36. Is any management staff plan documentation required?
<--- Score

37. What management staff plan improvements can be made?
<--- Score

38. How do you manage and improve your management staff plan work systems to deliver customer value and achieve organizational success and sustainability?
<--- Score

39. How will you know that a change is an improvement?
<--- Score

40. How will you recognize and celebrate results?
<--- Score

41. At what point will vulnerability assessments be performed once management staff plan is put into production (e.g., ongoing Risk Management after implementation)?
<--- Score

42. How does your organization evaluate strategic management staff plan success?
<--- Score

43. How do the management staff plan results compare with the performance of your competitors and other organizations with similar offerings?
<--- Score

44. If you could go back in time five years, what decision would you make differently? What is your best guess as to what decision you're making today you might regret five years from now?
<--- Score

45. What are the affordable management staff plan risks?
<--- Score

46. Who are the management staff plan decision-makers?
<--- Score

47. What error proofing will be done to address some of the discrepancies observed in the 'as is' process?
<--- Score

48. What were the criteria for evaluating a management staff plan pilot?
<--- Score

49. How scalable is your management staff plan solution?
<--- Score

50. What is the management staff plan's sustainability risk?
<--- Score

51. What risks do you need to manage?
<--- Score

52. What is management staff plan's impact on utilizing the best solution(s)?
<--- Score

53. Are risk management tasks balanced centrally and locally?
<--- Score

54. Is the measure of success for management staff plan understandable to a variety of people?
<--- Score

55. Which management staff plan solution is appropriate?
<--- Score

56. Is risk periodically assessed?
<--- Score

57. What tools do you use once you have decided on a management staff plan strategy and more

importantly how do you choose?
<--- Score

58. What do you want to improve?
<--- Score

59. Why improve in the first place?
<--- Score

60. How do you measure risk?
<--- Score

61. How can you better manage risk?
<--- Score

62. Risk events: what are the things that could go wrong?
<--- Score

63. What are the expected management staff plan results?
<--- Score

64. Which of the recognised risks out of all risks can be most likely transferred?
<--- Score

65. How do you define the solutions' scope?
<--- Score

66. What assumptions are made about the solution and approach?
<--- Score

67. What went well, what should change, what can improve?

<--- Score

68. Do you need to do a usability evaluation?
<--- Score

69. What needs improvement? Why?
<--- Score

70. What is the risk?
<--- Score

71. Who manages supplier risk management in your organization?
<--- Score

72. How will you know that you have improved?
<--- Score

73. What tools were most useful during the improve phase?
<--- Score

74. Can the solution be designed and implemented within an acceptable time period?
<--- Score

75. What improvements have been achieved?
<--- Score

76. What resources are required for the improvement efforts?
<--- Score

77. Is there any other management staff plan solution?
<--- Score

78. How does the team improve its work?
<--- Score

79. Can you identify any significant risks or exposures to management staff plan third- parties (vendors, service providers, alliance partners etc) that concern you?
<--- Score

80. Does the goal represent a desired result that can be measured?
<--- Score

81. Does a good decision guarantee a good outcome?
<--- Score

82. What current systems have to be understood and/ or changed?
<--- Score

83. Who should make the management staff plan decisions?
<--- Score

84. What is the implementation plan?
<--- Score

85. What tools were used to tap into the creativity and encourage 'outside the box' thinking?
<--- Score

86. How can you improve performance?
<--- Score

87. Is management staff plan documentation

maintained?
<--- Score

88. Who will be responsible for making the decisions to include or exclude requested changes once management staff plan is underway?
<--- Score

89. Are decisions made in a timely manner?
<--- Score

90. How significant is the improvement in the eyes of the end user?
<--- Score

91. Have you identified breakpoints and/or risk tolerances that will trigger broad consideration of a potential need for intervention or modification of strategy?
<--- Score

92. How do you go about comparing management staff plan approaches/solutions?
<--- Score

93. Who controls key decisions that will be made?
<--- Score

94. How do you link measurement and risk?
<--- Score

95. What is the magnitude of the improvements?
<--- Score

96. Do you cover the five essential competencies: Communication, Collaboration,Innovation,

Adaptability, and Leadership that improve an organizations ability to leverage the new management staff plan in a volatile global economy?
<--- Score

97. What are your current levels and trends in key measures or indicators of workforce and leader development?
<--- Score

98. What is management staff plan risk?
<--- Score

99. Is the management staff plan documentation thorough?
<--- Score

100. What communications are necessary to support the implementation of the solution?
<--- Score

101. Risk Identification: What are the possible risk events your organization faces in relation to management staff plan?
<--- Score

102. Is the management staff plan risk managed?
<--- Score

103. What are the implications of the one critical management staff plan decision 10 minutes, 10 months, and 10 years from now?
<--- Score

104. How risky is your organization?

<--- Score

105. What actually has to improve and by how much?
<--- Score

106. Who will be responsible for documenting the management staff plan requirements in detail?
<--- Score

107. Is supporting management staff plan documentation required?
<--- Score

108. Is the solution technically practical?
<--- Score

109. What tools were used to evaluate the potential solutions?
<--- Score

110. How can skill-level changes improve management staff plan?
<--- Score

111. What are the management staff plan security risks?
<--- Score

112. How do you keep improving management staff plan?
<--- Score

113. Who are the people involved in developing and implementing management staff plan?
<--- Score

114. Where do the management staff plan decisions reside?
<--- Score

115. Who are the management staff plan decision makers?
<--- Score

116. For decision problems, how do you develop a decision statement?
<--- Score

117. What area needs the greatest improvement?
<--- Score

118. What practices helps your organization to develop its capacity to recognize patterns?
<--- Score

119. How do you measure improved management staff plan service perception, and satisfaction?
<--- Score

120. For estimation problems, how do you develop an estimation statement?
<--- Score

121. Is the scope clearly documented?
<--- Score

122. How do you measure progress and evaluate training effectiveness?
<--- Score

123. What does the 'should be' process map/design look like?

<--- Score

124. Are the risks fully understood, reasonable and manageable?
<--- Score

125. Who do you report management staff plan results to?
<--- Score

126. What strategies for management staff plan improvement are successful?
<--- Score

127. How will you know when its improved?
<--- Score

128. What is the team's contingency plan for potential problems occurring in implementation?
<--- Score

129. How do you decide how much to remunerate an employee?
<--- Score

130. What can you do to improve?
<--- Score

Add up total points for this section:
_ _ _ _ _ = Total points for this section

Divided by: _ _ _ _ _ _ (number of statements answered) = _ _ _ _ _ _
Average score for this section

Transfer your score to the management

staff plan Index at the beginning of the
Self-Assessment.

CRITERION #6: CONTROL:

INTENT: Implement the practical solution. Maintain the performance and correct possible complications.

In my belief, the answer to this question is clearly defined:

5 Strongly Agree

4 Agree

3 Neutral

2 Disagree

1 Strongly Disagree

1. Will any special training be provided for results interpretation?
<--- Score

2. How do your controls stack up?
<--- Score

3. What is the best design framework for management staff plan organization now that, in a post industrial-

age if the top-down, command and control model is no longer relevant?
<--- Score

4. How do you spread information?
<--- Score

5. What do you measure to verify effectiveness gains?
<--- Score

6. How do controls support value?
<--- Score

7. Can you adapt and adjust to changing management staff plan situations?
<--- Score

8. What are the critical parameters to watch?
<--- Score

9. How will the process owner verify improvement in present and future sigma levels, process capabilities?
<--- Score

10. Are controls in place and consistently applied?
<--- Score

11. What is the standard for acceptable management staff plan performance?
<--- Score

12. What management staff plan standards are applicable?
<--- Score

13. What key inputs and outputs are being measured on an ongoing basis?
<--- Score

14. What are the performance and scale of the management staff plan tools?
<--- Score

15. Will your goals reflect your program budget?
<--- Score

16. Where do ideas that reach policy makers and planners as proposals for management staff plan strengthening and reform actually originate?
<--- Score

17. Has the management staff plan value of standards been quantified?
<--- Score

18. How do you plan for the cost of succession?
<--- Score

19. Who sets the management staff plan standards?
<--- Score

20. Are operating procedures consistent?
<--- Score

21. Do you monitor the management staff plan decisions made and fine tune them as they evolve?
<--- Score

22. Is there a recommended audit plan for routine surveillance inspections of management staff plan's gains?

<--- Score

23. Is a response plan in place for when the input, process, or output measures indicate an 'out-of-control' condition?
<--- Score

24. What are the key elements of your management staff plan performance improvement system, including your evaluation, organizational learning, and innovation processes?
<--- Score

25. How widespread is its use?
<--- Score

26. Will existing staff require re-training, for example, to learn new business processes?
<--- Score

27. Can support from partners be adjusted?
<--- Score

28. What do you stand for--and what are you against?
<--- Score

29. Implementation Planning: is a pilot needed to test the changes before a full roll out occurs?
<--- Score

30. How will new or emerging customer needs/ requirements be checked/communicated to orient the process toward meeting the new specifications and continually reducing variation?
<--- Score

31. Is there a documented and implemented monitoring plan?
<--- Score

32. Who controls critical resources?
<--- Score

33. How do you encourage people to take control and responsibility?
<--- Score

34. Do you monitor the effectiveness of your management staff plan activities?
<--- Score

35. Is there a transfer of ownership and knowledge to process owner and process team tasked with the responsibilities.
<--- Score

36. What are your results for key measures or indicators of the accomplishment of your management staff plan strategy and action plans, including building and strengthening core competencies?
<--- Score

37. What other areas of the group might benefit from the management staff plan team's improvements, knowledge, and learning?
<--- Score

38. Have new or revised work instructions resulted?
<--- Score

39. Is a response plan established and deployed?

<--- Score

40. How do you monitor usage and cost?
<--- Score

41. Who is going to spread your message?
<--- Score

42. What is the recommended frequency of auditing?
<--- Score

43. Is there a standardized process?
<--- Score

44. What is the control/monitoring plan?
<--- Score

45. What should the next improvement project be that is related to management staff plan?
<--- Score

46. Is there a control plan in place for sustaining improvements (short and long-term)?
<--- Score

47. Are documented procedures clear and easy to follow for the operators?
<--- Score

48. Who will be in control?
<--- Score

49. Are the planned controls in place?
<--- Score

50. Is the management staff plan test/monitoring cost

justified?
<--- Score

51. How do you select, collect, align, and integrate management staff plan data and information for tracking daily operations and overall organizational performance, including progress relative to strategic objectives and action plans?
<--- Score

52. Who is the management staff plan process owner?
<--- Score

53. How might the group capture best practices and lessons learned so as to leverage improvements?
<--- Score

54. Is knowledge gained on process shared and institutionalized?
<--- Score

55. How do you establish and deploy modified action plans if circumstances require a shift in plans and rapid execution of new plans?
<--- Score

56. What is your plan to assess your security risks?
<--- Score

57. How can you best use all of your knowledge repositories to enhance learning and sharing?
<--- Score

58. How is change control managed?
<--- Score

59. Does a troubleshooting guide exist or is it needed?
<--- Score

60. Has the improved process and its steps been standardized?
<--- Score

61. Is there documentation that will support the successful operation of the improvement?
<--- Score

62. Are new process steps, standards, and documentation ingrained into normal operations?
<--- Score

63. What are customers monitoring?
<--- Score

64. What can you control?
<--- Score

65. Are the management staff plan standards challenging?
<--- Score

66. Does management staff plan appropriately measure and monitor risk?
<--- Score

67. In the case of a management staff plan project, the criteria for the audit derive from implementation objectives, an audit of a management staff plan project involves assessing whether the recommendations outlined for implementation have been met, can you track that any management staff plan project is implemented as planned, and is it

working?
<--- Score

68. Does the response plan contain a definite closed loop continual improvement scheme (e.g., plan-do-check-act)?
<--- Score

69. Are suggested corrective/restorative actions indicated on the response plan for known causes to problems that might surface?
<--- Score

70. How do senior leaders actions reflect a commitment to the organizations management staff plan values?
<--- Score

71. How will the day-to-day responsibilities for monitoring and continual improvement be transferred from the improvement team to the process owner?
<--- Score

72. How will report readings be checked to effectively monitor performance?
<--- Score

73. Will the team be available to assist members in planning investigations?
<--- Score

74. Who has control over resources?
<--- Score

75. Are there documented procedures?

<--- Score

76. What is your theory of human motivation, and how does your compensation plan fit with that view?
<--- Score

77. What are the known security controls?
<--- Score

78. Do the viable solutions scale to future needs?
<--- Score

79. Are you measuring, monitoring and predicting management staff plan activities to optimize operations and profitability, and enhancing outcomes?
<--- Score

80. What do your reports reflect?
<--- Score

81. Act/Adjust: What Do you Need to Do Differently?
<--- Score

82. Is there a management staff plan Communication plan covering who needs to get what information when?
<--- Score

83. Does job training on the documented procedures need to be part of the process team's education and training?
<--- Score

84. How will you measure your QA plan's

effectiveness?

<--- Score

85. How will the process owner and team be able to hold the gains?

<--- Score

86. What quality tools were useful in the control phase?

<--- Score

87. What other systems, operations, processes, and infrastructures (hiring practices, staffing, training, incentives/rewards, metrics/dashboards/scorecards, etc.) need updates, additions, changes, or deletions in order to facilitate knowledge transfer and improvements?

<--- Score

88. How will management staff plan decisions be made and monitored?

<--- Score

89. How is management staff plan project cost planned, managed, monitored?

<--- Score

90. Are pertinent alerts monitored, analyzed and distributed to appropriate personnel?

<--- Score

91. What are you attempting to measure/monitor?

<--- Score

92. Is there an action plan in case of emergencies?

<--- Score

93. What should you measure to verify efficiency gains?
<--- Score

94. How likely is the current management staff plan plan to come in on schedule or on budget?
<--- Score

95. How do you plan on providing proper recognition and disclosure of supporting companies?
<--- Score

96. Is reporting being used or needed?
<--- Score

97. Is new knowledge gained imbedded in the response plan?
<--- Score

98. Does the management staff plan performance meet the customer's requirements?
<--- Score

99. Do the management staff plan decisions you make today help people and the planet tomorrow?
<--- Score

100. Are the planned controls working?
<--- Score

101. How will input, process, and output variables be checked to detect for sub-optimal conditions?
<--- Score

Add up total points for this section:

_____ = Total points for this section

Divided by: _____ (number of
statements answered) = _____
Average score for this section

Transfer your score to the management
staff plan Index at the beginning of the
Self-Assessment.

CRITERION #7: SUSTAIN:

INTENT: Retain the benefits.

In my belief, the answer to this question is clearly defined:

5 Strongly Agree

4 Agree

3 Neutral

2 Disagree

1 Strongly Disagree

1. How do you lead with management staff plan in mind?
<--- Score

2. Who is responsible for errors?
<--- Score

3. What are your most important goals for the strategic management staff plan objectives?
<--- Score

4. If you had to leave your organization for a year and the only communication you could have with employees/colleagues was a single paragraph, what would you write?
<--- Score

5. What role does communication play in the success or failure of a management staff plan project?
<--- Score

6. What is the range of capabilities?
<--- Score

7. How do you make it meaningful in connecting management staff plan with what users do day-to-day?
<--- Score

8. If you were responsible for initiating and implementing major changes in your organization, what steps might you take to ensure acceptance of those changes?
<--- Score

9. Where can you break convention?
<--- Score

10. If you find that you havent accomplished one of the goals for one of the steps of the management staff plan strategy, what will you do to fix it?
<--- Score

11. What are the challenges?
<--- Score

12. What are internal and external management

staff plan relations?
<--- Score

13. What trophy do you want on your mantle?
<--- Score

14. If there were zero limitations, what would you do differently?
<--- Score

15. Why is it important to have senior management support for a management staff plan project?
<--- Score

16. Who are the key stakeholders?
<--- Score

17. What are specific management staff plan rules to follow?
<--- Score

18. What is it like to work for you?
<--- Score

19. How do you foster innovation?
<--- Score

20. Do you have an implicit bias for capital investments over people investments?
<--- Score

21. Who, on the executive team or the board, has spoken to a customer recently?
<--- Score

22. When information truly is ubiquitous, when

reach and connectivity are completely global, when computing resources are infinite, and when a whole new set of impossibilities are not only possible, but happening, what will that do to your business?
<--- Score

23. If no one would ever find out about your accomplishments, how would you lead differently?
<--- Score

24. Political -is anyone trying to undermine this project?
<--- Score

25. Why should people listen to you?
<--- Score

26. What is your formula for success in management staff plan ?
<--- Score

27. Did your employees make progress today?
<--- Score

28. How do you know if you are successful?
<--- Score

29. Who is the main stakeholder, with ultimate responsibility for driving management staff plan forward?
<--- Score

30. Are you changing as fast as the world around you?
<--- Score

31. Which functions and people interact with the supplier and or customer?
<--- Score

32. In a project to restructure management staff plan outcomes, which stakeholders would you involve?
<--- Score

33. Ask yourself: how would you do this work if you only had one staff member to do it?
<--- Score

34. How do customers see your organization?
<--- Score

35. What are the barriers to increased management staff plan production?
<--- Score

36. If your customer were your grandmother, would you tell her to buy what you're selling?
<--- Score

37. How do you set management staff plan stretch targets and how do you get people to not only participate in setting these stretch targets but also that they strive to achieve these?
<--- Score

38. Do you know what you are doing? And who do you call if you don't?
<--- Score

39. How will you insure seamless interoperability of management staff plan moving forward?
<--- Score

40. Is there any existing management staff plan governance structure?
<--- Score

41. Who is responsible for management staff plan?
<--- Score

42. What is the purpose of management staff plan in relation to the mission?
<--- Score

43. Operational - will it work?
<--- Score

44. Is there a work around that you can use?
<--- Score

45. What projects are going on in the organization today, and what resources are those projects using from the resource pools?
<--- Score

46. At what moment would you think; Will I get fired?
<--- Score

47. If you weren't already in this business, would you enter it today? And if not, what are you going to do about it?
<--- Score

48. What is the overall business strategy?
<--- Score

49. How do you keep records, of what?

<--- Score

50. Who do you want your customers to become?
<--- Score

51. Do you think you know, or do you know you know ?
<--- Score

52. Are all key stakeholders present at all Structured Walkthroughs?
<--- Score

53. Is a management staff plan team work effort in place?
<--- Score

54. Has implementation been effective in reaching specified objectives so far?
<--- Score

55. Think of your management staff plan project, what are the main functions?
<--- Score

56. Is the management staff plan organization completing tasks effectively and efficiently?
<--- Score

57. What are the long-term management staff plan goals?
<--- Score

58. What will be the consequences to the stakeholder (financial, reputation etc) if management staff plan does not go ahead or fails

to deliver the objectives?
<--- Score

59. Which individuals, teams or departments will be involved in management staff plan?
<--- Score

60. To whom do you add value?
<--- Score

61. What is the recommended frequency of auditing?
<--- Score

62. What relationships among management staff plan trends do you perceive?
<--- Score

63. If you do not follow, then how to lead?
<--- Score

64. Who is on the team?
<--- Score

65. Which models, tools and techniques are necessary?
<--- Score

66. What would you recommend your friend do if he/she were facing this dilemma?
<--- Score

67. How do you assess the management staff plan pitfalls that are inherent in implementing it?
<--- Score

68. What are the short and long-term management

staff plan goals?

<--- Score

69. Will there be any necessary staff changes (redundancies or new hires)?

<--- Score

70. Can you maintain your growth without detracting from the factors that have contributed to your success?

<--- Score

71. What information is critical to your organization that your executives are ignoring?

<--- Score

72. Who else should you help?

<--- Score

73. Do you feel that more should be done in the management staff plan area?

<--- Score

74. How do you provide a safe environment -physically and emotionally?

<--- Score

75. Are the assumptions believable and achievable?

<--- Score

76. What management staff plan skills are most important?

<--- Score

77. Do you know who is a friend or a foe?

<--- Score

78. What are current management staff plan paradigms?
<--- Score

79. Are you relevant? Will you be relevant five years from now? Ten?
<--- Score

80. What are the success criteria that will indicate that management staff plan objectives have been met and the benefits delivered?
<--- Score

81. If you had to rebuild your organization without any traditional competitive advantages (i.e., no killer technology, promising research, innovative product/ service delivery model, etcetera), how would your people have to approach their work and collaborate together in order to create the necessary conditions for success?
<--- Score

82. Instead of going to current contacts for new ideas, what if you reconnected with dormant contacts--the people you used to know? If you were going reactivate a dormant tie, who would it be?
<--- Score

83. Are the criteria for selecting recommendations stated?
<--- Score

84. What management staff plan modifications can

you make work for you?
<--- Score

85. How do senior leaders deploy your organizations vision and values through your leadership system, to the workforce, to key suppliers and partners, and to customers and other stakeholders, as appropriate?
<--- Score

86. Why do and why don't your customers like your organization?
<--- Score

87. What should you stop doing?
<--- Score

88. What counts that you are not counting?
<--- Score

89. How will you motivate the stakeholders with the least vested interest?
<--- Score

90. Do you think management staff plan accomplishes the goals you expect it to accomplish?
<--- Score

91. What are your personal philosophies regarding management staff plan and how do they influence your work?
<--- Score

92. What is your competitive advantage?
<--- Score

93. What is the source of the strategies for management staff plan strengthening and reform?
<--- Score

94. What threat is management staff plan addressing?
<--- Score

95. How can you become more high-tech but still be high touch?
<--- Score

96. How do you proactively clarify deliverables and management staff plan quality expectations?
<--- Score

97. What trouble can you get into?
<--- Score

98. What are the essentials of internal management staff plan management?
<--- Score

99. What are the key enablers to make this management staff plan move?
<--- Score

100. What does your signature ensure?
<--- Score

101. What are the rules and assumptions your industry operates under? What if the opposite were true?
<--- Score

102. Is your basic point _____ or _____?
<--- Score

103. What are you trying to prove to yourself, and how might it be hijacking your life and business success?

<--- Score

104. How do you govern and fulfill your societal responsibilities?

<--- Score

105. What happens if you do not have enough funding?

<--- Score

106. What are the business goals management staff plan is aiming to achieve?

<--- Score

107. What is the kind of project structure that would be appropriate for your management staff plan project, should it be formal and complex, or can it be less formal and relatively simple?

<--- Score

108. What knowledge, skills and characteristics mark a good management staff plan project manager?

<--- Score

109. What management system can you use to leverage the management staff plan experience, ideas, and concerns of the people closest to the work to be done?

<--- Score

110. How do you determine the key elements that

affect management staff plan workforce satisfaction, how are these elements determined for different workforce groups and segments?

<--- Score

111. Would you rather sell to knowledgeable and informed customers or to uninformed customers?

<--- Score

112. What did you miss in the interview for the worst hire you ever made?

<--- Score

113. Who do we want your customers to become?

<--- Score

114. How do you manage management staff plan Knowledge Management (KM)?

<--- Score

115. How do you keep the momentum going?

<--- Score

116. Why is management staff plan important for you now?

<--- Score

117. Is management staff plan realistic, or are you setting yourself up for failure?

<--- Score

118. Who uses your product in ways you never expected?

<--- Score

119. Do you have the right people on the bus?

<--- Score

120. What is the craziest thing you can do?
<--- Score

121. Whom among your colleagues do you trust, and for what?
<--- Score

122. Are assumptions made in management staff plan stated explicitly?
<--- Score

123. How likely is it that a customer would recommend your company to a friend or colleague?
<--- Score

124. What are you challenging?
<--- Score

125. What is effective management staff plan?
<--- Score

126. How are you doing compared to your industry?
<--- Score

127. Do you say no to customers for no reason?
<--- Score

128. What happens when a new employee joins the organization?
<--- Score

129. What is an unauthorized commitment?
<--- Score

130. Marketing budgets are tighter, consumers are more skeptical, and social media has changed forever the way we talk about management staff plan, how do you gain traction?
<--- Score

131. How do you go about securing management staff plan?
<--- Score

132. Who are four people whose careers you have enhanced?
<--- Score

133. Can you do all this work?
<--- Score

134. How do you deal with management staff plan changes?
<--- Score

135. Who are your customers?
<--- Score

136. What is a feasible sequencing of reform initiatives over time?
<--- Score

137. How is implementation research currently incorporated into each of your goals?
<--- Score

138. Who will provide the final approval of management staff plan deliverables?
<--- Score

139. Why will customers want to buy your organizations products/services?
<--- Score

140. Who will be responsible for deciding whether management staff plan goes ahead or not after the initial investigations?
<--- Score

141. What happens at your organization when people fail?
<--- Score

142. How do you ensure that implementations of management staff plan products are done in a way that ensures safety?
<--- Score

143. What is the overall talent health of your organization as a whole at senior levels, and for each organization reporting to a member of the Senior Leadership Team?
<--- Score

144. Do you have past management staff plan successes?
<--- Score

145. How do you cross-sell and up-sell your management staff plan success?
<--- Score

146. What business benefits will management staff plan goals deliver if achieved?
<--- Score

147. Why not do management staff plan?
<--- Score

148. Can the schedule be done in the given time?
<--- Score

149. Do you see more potential in people than they do in themselves?
<--- Score

150. In the past year, what have you done (or could you have done) to increase the accurate perception of your company/brand as ethical and honest?
<--- Score

151. What one word do you want to own in the minds of your customers, employees, and partners?
<--- Score

152. What new services of functionality will be implemented next with management staff plan ?
<--- Score

153. How do you foster the skills, knowledge, talents, attributes, and characteristics you want to have?
<--- Score

154. In retrospect, of the projects that you pulled the plug on, what percent do you wish had been allowed to keep going, and what percent do you wish had ended earlier?
<--- Score

155. How do you transition from the baseline to the target?

<--- Score

156. How will you know that the management staff plan project has been successful?
<--- Score

157. Will it be accepted by users?
<--- Score

158. If you got fired and a new hire took your place, what would she do different?
<--- Score

159. What unique value proposition (UVP) do you offer?
<--- Score

160. Are you satisfied with your current role? If not, what is missing from it?
<--- Score

161. Who do you think the world wants your organization to be?
<--- Score

162. How do you stay inspired?
<--- Score

163. How can you negotiate management staff plan successfully with a stubborn boss, an irate client, or a deceitful coworker?
<--- Score

164. What are the potential basics of management staff plan fraud?
<--- Score

165. What could happen if you do not do it?
<--- Score

166. How do you accomplish your long range
management staff plan goals?
<--- Score

167. How long will it take to change?
<--- Score

168. How do you engage the workforce, in addition to
satisfying them?
<--- Score

169. Is maximizing management staff plan protection
the same as minimizing management staff plan loss?
<--- Score

**170. Are you / should you be revolutionary or
evolutionary?**
<--- Score

171. Are you paying enough attention to the partners
your company depends on to succeed?
<--- Score

172. What are the gaps in your knowledge and
experience?
<--- Score

173. What is the big management staff plan idea?
<--- Score

174. Do you have the right capabilities and capacities?
<--- Score

175. What would have to be true for the option on the table to be the best possible choice?
<--- Score

176. What have you done to protect your business from competitive encroachment?
<--- Score

177. Are you maintaining a past–present–future perspective throughout the management staff plan discussion?
<--- Score

178. How much contingency will be available in the budget?
<--- Score

179. Is there any reason to believe the opposite of my current belief?
<--- Score

180. What potential megatrends could make your business model obsolete?
<--- Score

181. Whose voice (department, ethnic group, women, older workers, etc) might you have missed hearing from in your company, and how might you amplify this voice to create positive momentum for your business?
<--- Score

182. What are the top 3 things at the forefront of your management staff plan agendas for the next 3 years?

<--- Score

183. What is the funding source for this project?
<--- Score

184. Do you have enough freaky customers in your portfolio pushing you to the limit day in and day out?
<--- Score

185. How will you ensure you get what you expected?
<--- Score

186. What is your management staff plan strategy?
<--- Score

187. How do you create buy-in?
<--- Score

188. What are strategies for increasing support and reducing opposition?
<--- Score

189. What goals did you miss?
<--- Score

190. How can you become the company that would put you out of business?
<--- Score

191. Is it economical; do you have the time and money?
<--- Score

192. How important is management staff plan to the user organizations mission?

<--- Score

193. What was the last experiment you ran?
<--- Score

194. What stupid rule would you most like to kill?
<--- Score

195. What are the usability implications of management staff plan actions?
<--- Score

196. Why should you adopt a management staff plan framework?
<--- Score

197. Is your strategy driving your strategy? Or is the way in which you allocate resources driving your strategy?
<--- Score

198. How do you maintain management staff plan's Integrity?
<--- Score

199. What is the estimated value of the project?
<--- Score

200. Who will determine interim and final deadlines?
<--- Score

Add up total points for this section:
_ _ _ _ _ = Total points for this section

Divided by: _ _ _ _ _ _ (number of
statements answered) = _ _ _ _ _ _

Average score for this section

Transfer your score to the management
staff plan Index at the beginning of the
Self-Assessment.

Management Staff Plan and Managing Projects, Criteria for Project Managers:

1.0 Initiating Process Group: Management Staff Plan

1. How well defined and documented were the Management Staff Plan project management processes you chose to use?

2. Mitigate. what will you do to minimize the impact should the risk event occur?

3. Which six sigma dmaic phase focuses on why and how defects and errors occur?

4. Were sponsors and decision makers available when needed outside regularly scheduled meetings?

5. Who is funding the Management Staff Plan project?

6. At which stage, in a typical Management Staff Plan project do stake holders have maximum influence?

7. Who is behind the Management Staff Plan project?

8. How well did the chosen processes fit the needs of the Management Staff Plan project?

9. Based on your Management Staff Plan project communication management plan, what worked well?

10. What do they need to know about the Management Staff Plan project?

11. The Management Staff Plan project you are managing has nine stakeholders. How many channel

of communications are there between corresponding stakeholders?

12. How should needs be met?

13. What technical work to do in each phase?

14. During which stage of Risk planning are risks prioritized based on probability and impact?

15. Are there resources to maintain and support the outcome of the Management Staff Plan project?

16. What areas does the group agree are the biggest success on the Management Staff Plan project?

17. Do you know if the Management Staff Plan project requires outside equipment or vendor resources?

18. What are the overarching issues of your organization?

19. How well did you do?

20. When will the Management Staff Plan project be done?

1.1 Project Charter: Management Staff Plan

21. Dependent Management Staff Plan projects: what Management Staff Plan projects must be underway or completed before this Management Staff Plan project can be successful?

22. How high should you set your goals?

23. Why have you chosen the aim you have set forth?

24. Are there special technology requirements?

25. What is the most common tool for helping define the detail?

26. If finished, on what date did it finish?

27. What metrics could you look at?

28. Customer: who are you doing the Management Staff Plan project for?

29. Strategic fit: what is the strategic initiative identifier for this Management Staff Plan project?

30. Are you building in-house ?

31. What are you trying to accomplish?

32. What changes can you make to improve?

33. When?

34. Who is the Management Staff Plan project Manager?

35. What is the purpose of the Management Staff Plan project?

36. Is it an improvement over existing products?

37. Management Staff Plan project deliverables: what is the Management Staff Plan project going to produce?

38. Run it as as a startup?

39. What is the business need?

40. What are some examples of a business case?

1.2 Stakeholder Register: Management Staff Plan

41. How much influence do they have on the Management Staff Plan project?

42. What opportunities exist to provide communications?

43. Who are the stakeholders?

44. What is the power of the stakeholder?

45. Who wants to talk about Security?

46. What are the major Management Staff Plan project milestones requiring communications or providing communications opportunities?

47. How will reports be created?

48. How big is the gap?

49. How should employers make voices heard?

50. Who is managing stakeholder engagement?

51. What & Why?

52. Is your organization ready for change?

1.3 Stakeholder Analysis Matrix: Management Staff Plan

53. Market demand?

54. Could any of your organizations weaknesses seriously threaten development?

55. Who can contribute financial or technical resources towards the work?

56. Who has control over whom?

57. If you can not fix it, how do you do it differently?

58. Where are mitigation costs factored in?

59. Price, value, quality?

60. New markets, vertical, horizontal?

61. Global influences?

62. Gaps in capabilities?

63. Are there people who ise voices or interests in the issue may not be heard?

64. What makes a person a stakeholder?

65. What is the stakeholders power and status in relation to the Management Staff Plan project?

66. Arena: in what fields are the actors active, where are they present?

67. Identify the stakeholders levels most frequently used –or at least sought– in your Management Staff Plan projects and for which purpose?

68. Loss of key staff?

69. Volumes, production, economies?

70. What is your Risk Management?

71. What is social & public accountability ?

72. What is relationship with the Management Staff Plan project?

2.0 Planning Process Group: Management Staff Plan

73. How are the principles of aid effectiveness (ownership, alignment, management for development results and mutual responsibility) being applied in the Management Staff Plan project?

74. Explanation: is what the Management Staff Plan project intents to solve a hard question?

75. What good practices or successful experiences or transferable examples have been identified?

76. Is your organization showing technical capacity and leadership commitment to keep working with the Management Staff Plan project and to repeat it?

77. What business situation is being addressed?

78. What do they need to know about the Management Staff Plan project?

79. What should you do next?

80. How many days can task X be late in starting without affecting the Management Staff Plan project completion date?

81. Why do it Management Staff Plan projects fail?

82. Contingency planning. if a risk event occurs, what will you do?

83. What are the different approaches to building the WBS?

84. When will the Management Staff Plan project be done?

85. Just how important is your work to the overall success of the Management Staff Plan project?

86. If action is called for, what form should it take?

87. Product breakdown structure (pbs): what is the Management Staff Plan project result or product, and how should it look like, what are its parts?

88. How can you tell when you are done?

89. Are there efficient coordination mechanisms to avoid overloading the counterparts, participating stakeholders?

90. To what extent has the intervention strategy been adapted to the areas of intervention in which it is being implemented?

91. To what extent are the participating departments coordinating with each other?

2.1 Project Management Plan: Management Staff Plan

92. Are alternatives safe, functional, constructible, economical, reasonable and sustainable?

93. Does the implementation plan have an appropriate division of responsibilities?

94. What went right?

95. Is mitigation authorized or recommended?

96. What are the known stakeholder requirements?

97. What is the justification?

98. What would you do differently what did not work?

99. Are cost risk analysis methods applied to develop contingencies for the estimated total Management Staff Plan project costs?

100. Will you add a schedule and diagram?

101. What would you do differently?

102. What should you drop in order to add something new?

103. What is Management Staff Plan project scope management?

104. What happened during the process that you found interesting?

105. Are there any Client staffing expectations?

106. Has the selected plan been formulated using cost effectiveness and incremental analysis techniques?

107. Was the peer (technical) review of the cost estimates duly coordinated with the cost estimate center of expertise and addressed in the review documentation and certification?

108. When is the Management Staff Plan project management plan created?

109. What are the training needs?

2.2 Scope Management Plan: Management Staff Plan

110. Has the scope management document been updated and distributed to help prevent scope creep?

111. Pop quiz – which are the same inputs as in scope planning?

112. Are procurement deliverables arriving on time and to specification?

113. Are multiple estimation methods being employed?

114. Have Management Staff Plan project team accountabilities & responsibilities been clearly defined?

115. Have all unresolved risks been documented?

116. Have Management Staff Plan project success criteria been defined?

117. Who is responsible for monitoring the Management Staff Plan project scope to ensure the Management Staff Plan project remains within the scope baseline?

118. Are calculations and results of analyzes essentially correct?

119. Have the procedures for identifying budget

variances been followed?

120. Assess the expected stability of the scope of this Management Staff Plan project how likely is it to change, how frequently, and by how much?

121. Are staff skills known and available for each task?

122. Have external dependencies been captured in the schedule?

123. Have adequate resources been provided by management to ensure Management Staff Plan project success?

124. Have the procedures for identifying variances from estimates & adjusting the detailed work program been followed?

125. Are agendas created for each meeting with meeting objectives, meeting topics, invitee list, and action items from past meetings?

126. Have all involved Management Staff Plan project stakeholders and work groups committed to the Management Staff Plan project?

127. Function of the configuration control board?

128. Product – what are you trying to accomplish and how will you know when you are finished?

129. What is the relative power of the Management Staff Plan project manager?

2.3 Requirements Management Plan: Management Staff Plan

130. How often will the reporting occur?

131. In case of software development; Should you have a test for each code module?

132. Is the system software (non-operating system) new to the IT Management Staff Plan project team?

133. What is the earliest finish date for this Management Staff Plan project if it is scheduled to start on ...?

134. Are actual resource expenditures versus planned still acceptable?

135. Is the user satisfied?

136. What went wrong?

137. Who will finally present the work or product(s) for acceptance?

138. Will you use an assessment of the Management Staff Plan project environment as a tool to discover risk to the requirements process?

139. Who came up with this requirement?

140. How will unresolved questions be handled once approval has been obtained?

141. How will the information be distributed?

142. Will the contractors involved take full responsibility?

143. What is a problem?

144. Subject to change control?

145. Define the help desk model. who will take full responsibility?

146. Who will do the reporting and to whom will reports be delivered?

147. Is there formal agreement on who has authority to approve a change in requirements?

148. How will you communicate scheduled tasks to other team members?

149. If it exists, where is it housed?

2.4 Requirements Documentation: Management Staff Plan

150. Who is involved?

151. Basic work/business process; high-level, what is being touched?

152. What are current process problems?

153. What images does it conjure?

154. Does your organization restrict technical alternatives?

155. What will be the integration problems?

156. Has requirements gathering uncovered information that would necessitate changes?

157. How do you get the user to tell you what they want?

158. How to document system requirements?

159. How much testing do you need to do to prove that your system is safe?

160. What is a show stopper in the requirements?

161. Can the requirement be changed without a large impact on other requirements?

162. What happens when requirements are wrong?

163. What is the risk associated with the technology?

164. Consistency. are there any requirements conflicts?

165. What is your Elevator Speech?

166. Who provides requirements?

167. Do your constraints stand?

168. Is the origin of the requirement clearly stated?

169. Validity. does the system provide the functions which best support the customers needs?

2.5 Requirements Traceability Matrix: Management Staff Plan

170. What are the chronologies, contingencies, consequences, criteria?

171. What percentage of Management Staff Plan projects are producing traceability matrices between requirements and other work products?

172. Describe the process for approving requirements so they can be added to the traceability matrix and Management Staff Plan project work can be performed. Will the Management Staff Plan project requirements become approved in writing?

173. Will you use a Requirements Traceability Matrix?

174. Do you have a clear understanding of all subcontracts in place?

175. Is there a requirements traceability process in place?

176. Why do you manage scope?

177. What is the WBS?

178. How do you manage scope?

179. Why use a WBS?

180. How will it affect the stakeholders personally in

career?

181. How small is small enough?

2.6 Project Scope Statement: Management Staff Plan

182. Identify how your team and you will create the Management Staff Plan project scope statement and the work breakdown structure (WBS). Document how you will create the Management Staff Plan project scope statement and WBS, and make sure you answer the following questions: In defining Management Staff Plan project scope and the WBS, will you and your Management Staff Plan project team be using methods defined by your organization, methods defined by the Management Staff Plan project management office (PMO), or other methods?

183. Were key Management Staff Plan project stakeholders brought into the Management Staff Plan project Plan?

184. Will statistics related to QA be collected, trends analyzed, and problems raised as issues?

185. Did your Management Staff Plan project ask for this?

186. Elements of scope management that deal with concept development ?

187. What actions will be taken to mitigate the risk?

188. Is the plan for Management Staff Plan project resources adequate?

189. If you were to write a list of what should not be included in the scope statement, what are the things that you would recommend be described as out-of-scope?

190. Are the meetings set up to have assigned note takers that will add action/issues to the issue list?

191. What are the defined meeting materials?

192. Has the Management Staff Plan project scope statement been reviewed as part of the baseline process?

193. Does the scope statement still need some clarity?

194. Any new risks introduced or old risks impacted. Are there issues that could affect the existing requirements for the result, service, or product if the scope changes?

195. Is the change control process documented and on file?

196. Will the risk status be reported to management on a regular and frequent basis?

197. Once its defined, what is the stability of the Management Staff Plan project scope?

198. Are there issues that could affect the existing requirements for the result, service, or product if the scope changes?

199. Is the plan under configuration management?

2.7 Assumption and Constraint Log: Management Staff Plan

200. Is the amount of effort justified by the anticipated value of forming a new process?

201. Are there unnecessary steps that are creating bottlenecks and/or causing people to wait?

202. Should factors be unpredictable over time?

203. Would known impacts serve as impediments?

204. Are there procedures in place to effectively manage interdependencies with other Management Staff Plan projects / systems?

205. Do documented requirements exist for all critical components and areas, including technical, business, interfaces, performance, security and conversion requirements?

206. What would you gain if you spent time working to improve this process?

207. Is the steering committee active in Management Staff Plan project oversight?

208. What worked well?

209. Is there documentation of system capability requirements, data requirements, environment requirements, security requirements, and computer

and hardware requirements?

210. After observing execution of process, is it in compliance with the documented Plan?

211. Have all stakeholders been identified?

212. What strengths do you have?

213. Have you eliminated all duplicative tasks or manual efforts, where appropriate?

214. What weaknesses do you have?

215. Has a Management Staff Plan project Communications Plan been developed?

216. Are formal code reviews conducted?

217. Is this model reasonable?

218. How do you design an auditing system?

219. How can constraints be violated?

2.8 Work Breakdown Structure: Management Staff Plan

220. How big is a work-package?

221. Do you need another level?

222. When do you stop?

223. When would you develop a Work Breakdown Structure?

224. How far down?

225. Why would you develop a Work Breakdown Structure?

226. Is it a change in scope?

227. Where does it take place?

228. Is it still viable?

229. What is the probability that the Management Staff Plan project duration will exceed xx weeks?

230. When does it have to be done?

231. Can you make it?

232. Who has to do it?

233. Is the work breakdown structure (wbs) defined

and is the scope of the Management Staff Plan project clear with assigned deliverable owners?

234. How will you and your Management Staff Plan project team define the Management Staff Plan projects scope and work breakdown structure?

235. Why is it useful?

236. How much detail?

237. How many levels?

2.9 WBS Dictionary: Management Staff Plan

238. Are control accounts opened and closed based on the start and completion of work contained therein?

239. Are there procedures for monitoring action items and corrective actions to the point of resolution and are corresponding procedures being followed?

240. Is subcontracted work defined and identified to the appropriate subcontractor within the proper WBS element?

241. What size should a work package be?

242. Does the contractors system provide unit costs, equivalent unit or lot costs in terms of labor, material, other direct, and indirect costs?

243. Do work packages reflect the actual way in which the work will be done and are they meaningful products or management-oriented subdivisions of a higher level element of work?

244. Where engineering standards or other internal work measurement systems are used, is there a formal relationship between corresponding values and work package budgets?

245. Are all elements of indirect expense identified to overhead cost budgets of Management Staff Plan

projections?

246. Are estimates of costs at completion generated in a rational, consistent manner?

247. Are retroactive changes to BCWS and BCWP prohibited except for correction of errors or for normal accounting adjustments?

248. The Management Staff Plan projected business base for each period?

249. Should you have a test for each code module?

250. Changes in the nature of the overhead requirements?

251. Are the bases and rates for allocating costs from each indirect pool consistently applied?

252. Actual cost of work performed?

253. All cwbs elements specified for external reporting?

254. Are data elements summarized through the functional organizational structure for progressively higher levels of management?

255. Are current budgets resulting from changes to the authorized work and/or internal replanning, reconcilable to original budgets for specified reporting items?

256. Software specification, development, integration, and testing, licenses ?

2.10 Schedule Management Plan: Management Staff Plan

257. Are target dates established for each milestone deliverable?

258. Are all activities logically sequenced?

259. Has the Management Staff Plan project manager been identified?

260. Is stakeholder involvement adequate?

261. Are software metrics formally captured, analyzed and used as a basis for other Management Staff Plan project estimates?

262. Is there a Steering Committee in place?

263. Are all activities captured and do they address all approved work scope in the Management Staff Plan project baseline?

264. Is there an onboarding process in place?

265. Are the appropriate IT resources adequate to meet planned commitments?

266. Are the processes for schedule assessment and analysis defined?

267. Are the Management Staff Plan project team members located locally to the users/stakeholders?

268. What happens if a warning is triggered?

269. Does the schedule have reasonable float?

270. Has a resource management plan been created?

271. Are decisions captured in a decisions log?

272. How do you manage time?

273. Quality assurance overheads?

274. Is funded schedule margin reasonable and logically distributed?

275. Has process improvement efforts been completed before requirements efforts begin?

2.11 Activity List: Management Staff Plan

276. What is the probability the Management Staff Plan project can be completed in xx weeks?

277. When do the individual activities need to start and finish?

278. How will it be performed?

279. The wbs is developed as part of a joint planning session. and how do you know that youhave done this right?

280. When will the work be performed?

281. Who will perform the work?

282. How can the Management Staff Plan project be displayed graphically to better visualize the activities?

283. How do you determine the late start (LS) for each activity?

284. Are the required resources available or need to be acquired?

285. Where will it be performed?

286. What went well?

287. Should you include sub-activities?

288. For other activities, how much delay can be tolerated?

289. What is the LF and LS for each activity?

290. What is your organizations history in doing similar activities?

291. How should ongoing costs be monitored to try to keep the Management Staff Plan project within budget?

292. Is infrastructure setup part of your Management Staff Plan project?

293. What will be performed?

294. In what sequence?

2.12 Activity Attributes: Management Staff Plan

295. How many resources do you need to complete the work scope within a limit of X number of days?

296. Activity: fair or not fair?

297. Were there other ways you could have organized the data to achieve similar results?

298. What is the general pattern here?

299. Can more resources be added?

300. Activity: what is Missing?

301. Where else does it apply?

302. Do you feel very comfortable with your prediction?

303. Does your organization of the data change its meaning?

304. Can you re-assign any activities to another resource to resolve an over-allocation?

305. Have constraints been applied to the start and finish milestones for the phases?

306. Resource is assigned to?

307. What activity do you think you should spend the most time on?

308. Time for overtime?

309. How much activity detail is required?

310. Have you identified the Activity Leveling Priority code value on each activity?

2.13 Milestone List: Management Staff Plan

311. How soon can the activity finish?

312. What specific improvements did you make to the Management Staff Plan project proposal since the previous time?

313. How late can the activity start?

314. Own known vulnerabilities?

315. Continuity, supply chain robustness?

316. Sustainable financial backing?

317. Milestone pages should display the UserID of the person who added the milestone. Does a report or query exist that provides this audit information?

318. What date will the task finish?

319. Which path is the critical path?

320. Insurmountable weaknesses?

321. Sustaining internal capabilities?

322. Identify critical paths (one or more) and which activities are on the critical path?

323. Do you foresee any technical risks or

developmental challenges?

324. Reliability of data, plan predictability?

325. Marketing - reach, distribution, awareness?

326. How soon can the activity start?

327. How late can each activity be finished and started?

328. Environmental effects?

2.14 Network Diagram: Management Staff Plan

329. If a current contract exists, can you provide the vendor name, contract start, and contract expiration date?

330. Which type of network diagram allows you to depict four types of dependencies?

331. What are the Key Success Factors?

332. Where do you schedule uncertainty time?

333. What activities must occur simultaneously with this activity?

334. Are the required resources available?

335. How confident can you be in your milestone dates and the delivery date?

336. What to do and When?

337. What activity must be completed immediately before this activity can start?

338. What is the completion time?

339. Are you on time?

340. What is the probability of completing the Management Staff Plan project in less that xx days?

341. What are the Major Administrative Issues?

342. Planning: who, how long, what to do?

343. If x is long, what would be the completion time if you break x into two parallel parts of y weeks and z weeks?

344. What controls the start and finish of a job?

345. What job or jobs could run concurrently?

346. What is the lowest cost to complete this Management Staff Plan project in xx weeks?

347. What job or jobs follow it?

2.15 Activity Resource Requirements: Management Staff Plan

348. How do you handle petty cash?

349. What are constraints that you might find during the Human Resource Planning process?

350. When does monitoring begin?

351. Other support in specific areas?

352. Do you use tools like decomposition and rolling-wave planning to produce the activity list and other outputs?

353. Organizational Applicability?

354. Which logical relationship does the PDM use most often?

355. How many signatures do you require on a check and does this match what is in your policy and procedures?

356. Is there anything planned that does not need to be here?

357. Are there unresolved issues that need to be addressed?

358. Why do you do that?

359. What is the Work Plan Standard?

360. Anything else?

2.16 Resource Breakdown Structure: Management Staff Plan

361. How difficult will it be to do specific activities on this Management Staff Plan project?

362. Why do you do it?

363. What is the number one predictor of a groups productivity?

364. Who will use the system?

365. Any changes from stakeholders?

366. Which resources should be in the resource pool?

367. Who delivers the information?

368. How should the information be delivered?

369. What is each stakeholders desired outcome for the Management Staff Plan project?

370. When do they need the information?

371. What defines a successful Management Staff Plan project?

372. The list could probably go on, but, the thing that you would most like to know is, How long & How much?

373. Why is this important?

374. What defines a successful Management Staff Plan project?

375. What is the purpose of assigning and documenting responsibility?

376. Who needs what information?

377. Changes based on input from stakeholders?

2.17 Activity Duration Estimates: Management Staff Plan

378. Are operational definitions created to identify quality measurement criteria for specific activities?

379. Does the software appear easy to learn?

380. Does a process exist to identify which qualified resources may be attainable?

381. Will it help in finding or retaining employees?

382. Do they make sense?

383. Are team building activities completed to improve team performance?

384. Where do schedules come from?

385. Will the new application be developed using existing hardware, software, and networks?

386. Is the cost performance monitored to identify variances from the plan?

387. Is evaluation criteria defined to rate proposals?

388. Does the case present a realistic scenario?

389. Could it have been avoided?

390. Consider the history of modern quality

management. How have experts such as Deming, Juran, Crosby, and Taguchi affected the quality movement and todays use of Six Sigma?

391. How can others help Management Staff Plan project managers understand your organizational context for Management Staff Plan projects?

392. Which skills do you think are most important for an information technology Management Staff Plan project manager?

393. What is the duration of the critical path for this Management Staff Plan project?

394. Which does one need in order to complete schedule development?

395. Is training acquired to enhance the skills, knowledge and capabilities of the Management Staff Plan project team?

396. Are Management Staff Plan project results verified and Management Staff Plan project documents archived?

397. Is corrective action taken to bring Management Staff Plan project performance into line with the Management Staff Plan project plan?

2.18 Duration Estimating Worksheet: Management Staff Plan

398. What are the critical bottleneck activities?

399. Science = process: remember the scientific method?

400. Why estimate time and cost?

401. What is next?

402. Is the Management Staff Plan project responsive to community need?

403. Do any colleagues have experience with your organization and/or RFPs?

404. What info is needed?

405. Why estimate costs?

406. Done before proceeding with this activity or what can be done concurrently?

407. How should ongoing costs be monitored to try to keep the Management Staff Plan project within budget?

408. Does the Management Staff Plan project provide innovative ways for stakeholders to overcome obstacles or deliver better outcomes?

409. Small or large Management Staff Plan project?

410. Can the Management Staff Plan project be constructed as planned?

411. What utility impacts are there?

412. Is this operation cost effective?

413. Is a construction detail attached (to aid in explanation)?

414. What is your role?

2.19 Project Schedule: Management Staff Plan

415. Activity charts and bar charts are graphical representations of a Management Staff Plan project schedule ...how do they differ?

416. What does that mean?

417. Why do you need schedules?

418. If there are any qualifying green components to this Management Staff Plan project, what portion of the total Management Staff Plan project cost is green?

419. To what degree is do you feel the entire team was committed to the Management Staff Plan project schedule?

420. Are key risk mitigation strategies added to the Management Staff Plan project schedule?

421. Why do you think schedule issues often cause the most conflicts on Management Staff Plan projects?

422. Are there activities that came from a template or previous Management Staff Plan project that are not applicable on this phase of this Management Staff Plan project?

423. Your Management Staff Plan project management plan results in a Management Staff Plan project schedule that is too long. If the Management

Staff Plan project network diagram cannot change and you have extra personnel resources, what is the BEST thing to do?

424. Why time management?

425. Is there a Schedule Management Plan that establishes the criteria and activities for developing, monitoring and controlling the Management Staff Plan project schedule?

426. Why is this particularly bad?

427. Are you working on the right risks?

428. Are procedures defined by which the Management Staff Plan project schedule may be changed?

429. Are quality inspections and review activities listed in the Management Staff Plan project schedule(s)?

430. How can slack be negative?

431. How effectively were issues able to be resolved without impacting the Management Staff Plan project Schedule or Budget?

2.20 Cost Management Plan: Management Staff Plan

432. Are key risk mitigation strategies added to the Management Staff Plan project schedule?

433. Are vendor contract reports, reviews and visits conducted periodically?

434. Does the schedule include Management Staff Plan project management time and change request analysis time?

435. Resources – how will human resources be scheduled during each phase of the Management Staff Plan project?

436. Change types and category – What are the types of changes and what are the techniques to report and control changes?

437. Is the quality assurance team identified?

438. Are software metrics formally captured, analyzed and used as a basis for other Management Staff Plan project estimates?

439. Have activity relationships and interdependencies within tasks been adequately identified?

440. Is there an issues management plan in place?

441. Management Staff Plan project definition & scope?

442. The definition of the Management Staff Plan project scope what needs to be accomplished?

443. Is a payment system in place with proper reviews and approvals?

444. Similar Management Staff Plan projects?

445. Vac -variance at completion, how much over/ under budget do you expect to be?

446. Was the scope definition used in task sequencing?

447. Mitigation – based on the action, cost and probability of success, will the mitigation be made?

448. Have process improvement efforts been completed before requirements efforts begin?

449. Is it standard practice to formally commit stakeholders to the Management Staff Plan project via agreements?

450. Is pert / critical path or equivalent methodology being used?

2.21 Activity Cost Estimates: Management Staff Plan

451. Why do you manage cost?

452. How do you do activity recasts?

453. What were things that you did well, and could improve, and how?

454. What were things that you need to improve?

455. How Award?

456. Was it performed on time?

457. What makes a good activity description?

458. What defines a successful Management Staff Plan project?

459. Estimated cost?

460. What areas does the group agree are the biggest success on the Management Staff Plan project?

461. Were you satisfied with the work?

462. What is procurement?

463. Scope statement only direct or indirect costs as well?

464. When do you enter into PPM?

465. Can you delete activities or make them inactive?

466. How difficult will it be to do specific tasks on the Management Staff Plan project?

467. Were decisions made in a timely manner?

468. Would you hire them again?

469. Can you change your activities?

2.22 Cost Estimating Worksheet: Management Staff Plan

470. Value pocket identification & quantification what are value pockets?

471. Who is best positioned to know and assist in identifying corresponding factors?

472. Does the Management Staff Plan project provide innovative ways for stakeholders to overcome obstacles or deliver better outcomes?

473. What will others want?

474. Can a trend be established from historical performance data on the selected measure and are the criteria for using trend analysis or forecasting methods met?

475. What can be included?

476. Will the Management Staff Plan project collaborate with the local community and leverage resources?

477. Is it feasible to establish a control group arrangement?

478. What is the purpose of estimating?

479. What costs are to be estimated?

480. Ask: are others positioned to know, are others credible, and will others cooperate?

481. What is the estimated labor cost today based upon this information?

482. How will the results be shared and to whom?

483. What additional Management Staff Plan project(s) could be initiated as a result of this Management Staff Plan project?

484. Identify the timeframe necessary to monitor progress and collect data to determine how the selected measure has changed?

485. Is the Management Staff Plan project responsive to community need?

486. What happens to any remaining funds not used?

2.23 Cost Baseline: Management Staff Plan

487. Should a more thorough impact analysis be conducted?

488. Does the suggested change request represent a desired enhancement to the products functionality?

489. Has the Management Staff Plan projected annual cost to operate and maintain the product(s) or service(s) been approved and funded?

490. Have the lessons learned been filed with the Management Staff Plan project Management Office?

491. Have all the product or service deliverables been accepted by the customer?

492. On time?

493. How do you manage cost?

494. What deliverables come first?

495. Is there anything unique in this Management Staff Plan projects scope statement that will affect resources?

496. Have all approved changes to the schedule baseline been identified and impact on the Management Staff Plan project documented?

497. Review your risk triggers -have your risks changed?

498. Impact to environment?

499. What does a good WBS NOT look like?

500. Is there anything you need from upper management in order to be successful?

501. Is the cr within Management Staff Plan project scope?

502. What can go wrong?

503. Does a process exist for establishing a cost baseline to measure Management Staff Plan project performance?

504. On budget?

2.24 Quality Management Plan: Management Staff Plan

505. How does your organization maintain a safe and healthy work environment?

506. What key performance indicators does your organization use to measure, manage, and improve key processes?

507. Is a component/condition present?

508. How is staff informed of proper reporting methods?

509. How are new requirements or changes to requirements identified?

510. Is staff trained on the software technologies that are being used on the Management Staff Plan project?

511. How do you document and correct nonconformances?

512. How is staff trained on the recording of field notes?

513. What else should you do now?

514. How are senior leaders, employees, and your organization involved in supporting the community?

515. What process do you use to minimize errors, defects, and rework?

516. How are calibration records kept?

517. Can it be done better?

518. Sampling part of task?

519. What are the established criteria that sampling / testing data are compared against?

520. Does the program use modeling in the permitting or decision-making processes?

521. How does your organization design processes to ensure others meet customer and others requirements?

522. Have all necessary approvals been obtained?

523. Is there a Quality Management Plan?

524. Are you following the quality standards?

2.25 Quality Metrics: Management Staff Plan

525. Why is now the time for quality metrics?

526. Which data do others need in one place to target areas of improvement?

527. What happens if you get an abnormal result?

528. Does risk analysis documentation meet standards?

529. Did evaluation start on time?

530. What metrics are important and most beneficial to measure?

531. How do you know if everyone is trying to improve the right things?

532. What is the benchmark?

533. When will the Final Guidance will be issued?

534. What are your organizations next steps?

535. Did the team meet the Management Staff Plan project success criteria documented in the Quality Metrics Matrix?

536. Is there a set of procedures to capture, analyze and act on quality metrics?

537. What about still open problems?

538. Has risk analysis been adequately reviewed?

539. What documentation is required?

540. How do you calculate such metrics?

541. What forces exist that would cause them to change?

542. Were quality attributes reported?

543. What can manufacturing professionals do to ensure quality is seen as an integral part of the entire product lifecycle?

544. Which report did you use to create the data you are submitting?

2.26 Process Improvement Plan: Management Staff Plan

545. What personnel are the change agents for your initiative?

546. Are you making progress on the improvement framework?

547. What actions are needed to address the problems and achieve the goals?

548. Are you making progress on the goals?

549. What personnel are the sponsors for that initiative?

550. Does explicit definition of the measures exist?

551. Where do you want to be?

552. Why do you want to achieve the goal?

553. If a process improvement framework is being used, which elements will help the problems and goals listed?

554. What personnel are the coaches for your initiative?

555. Are you meeting the quality standards?

556. Does your process ensure quality?

557. Are you making progress on your improvement plan?

558. Who should prepare the process improvement action plan?

559. To elicit goal statements, do you ask a question such as, What do you want to achieve?

560. Management commitment at all levels?

561. Has a process guide to collect the data been developed?

562. How do you measure?

563. Where are you now?

564. Why quality management?

2.27 Responsibility Assignment Matrix: Management Staff Plan

565. What does wbs accomplish?

566. What cost control tool do many experts say is crucial to Management Staff Plan project management?

567. How many people do you need?

568. What materials and procurements needed?

569. Which Management Staff Plan project management knowledge area is least mature?

570. Does each activity-deliverable have exactly one Accountable responsibility, so that accountability is clear and decisions can be made quickly?

571. What are the assigned resources?

572. The already stated responsible for overhead performance control of related costs?

573. What travel needed?

574. Does the contractors system provide unit or lot costs when applicable?

575. Are data elements reconcilable between internal summary reports and reports forwarded to stakeholders?

576. Why cost benefit analysis?

577. Do all the identified groups or people really need to be consulted?

578. Are indirect costs accumulated for comparison with the corresponding budgets?

579. Does the contractor use objective results, design reviews and tests to trace schedule performance?

580. If a role has only Signing-off, or only Communicating responsibility and has no Performing, Accountable, or Monitoring responsibility, is it necessary?

581. The staff interests – is the group or the person interested in working for this Management Staff Plan project?

2.28 Roles and Responsibilities: Management Staff Plan

582. Do the values and practices inherent in the culture of your organization foster or hinder the process?

583. Are your budgets supportive of a culture of quality data?

584. Are governance roles and responsibilities documented?

585. What expectations were met?

586. Be specific; avoid generalities. Thank you and great work alone are insufficient. What exactly do you appreciate and why?

587. What areas would you highlight for changes or improvements?

588. What should you highlight for improvement?

589. Once the responsibilities are defined for the Management Staff Plan project, have the deliverables, roles and responsibilities been clearly communicated to every participant?

590. Was the expectation clearly communicated?

591. Influence: what areas of organizational decision making are you able to influence when you do not

have authority to make the final decision?

592. What areas of supervision are challenging for you?

593. Required skills, knowledge, experience?

594. Have you ever been a part of this team?

595. Once the responsibilities are defined for the Management Staff Plan project, have the deliverables, roles and responsibilities been clearly communicated to every participant?

596. What expectations were NOT met?

597. Are the quality assurance functions and related roles and responsibilities clearly defined?

598. Accountabilities: what are the roles and responsibilities of individual team members?

599. Who is responsible for implementation activities and where will the functions, roles and responsibilities be defined?

600. Is there a training program in place for stakeholders covering expectations, roles and responsibilities and any addition knowledge others need to be good stakeholders?

2.29 Human Resource Management Plan: Management Staff Plan

601. Were stakeholders aware and supportive of the principles and practices of modern cost estimation?

602. Is Management Staff Plan project work proceeding in accordance with the original Management Staff Plan project schedule?

603. Are the right people being attracted and retained to meet the future challenges?

604. Has your organization readiness assessment been conducted?

605. Are corrective actions and variances reported?

606. Are people motivated to meet the current and future challenges?

607. Is documentation created for communication with the suppliers and Vendors?

608. Are milestone deliverables effectively tracked and compared to Management Staff Plan project plan?

609. Are meeting minutes captured and sent out after the meeting?

610. Who needs training?

611. Has a provision been made to reassess Management Staff Plan project risks at various Management Staff Plan project stages?

612. Are Management Staff Plan project leaders committed to this Management Staff Plan project full time?

613. Is it possible to track all classes of Management Staff Plan project work (e.g. scheduled, un-scheduled, defect repair, etc.)?

614. Are the quality tools and methods identified in the Quality Plan appropriate to the Management Staff Plan project?

615. Has the Management Staff Plan project scope been baselined?

616. Are internal Management Staff Plan project status meetings held at reasonable intervals?

2.30 Communications Management Plan: Management Staff Plan

617. What steps can you take for a positive relationship?

618. In your work, how much time is spent on stakeholder identification?

619. How is this initiative related to other portfolios, programs, or Management Staff Plan projects?

620. Are you constantly rushing from meeting to meeting?

621. Are there common objectives between the team and the stakeholder?

622. Who have you worked with in past, similar initiatives?

623. Do you have members of your team responsible for certain stakeholders?

624. Timing: when do the effects of the communication take place?

625. How often do you engage with stakeholders?

626. Are the stakeholders getting the information others need, are others consulted, are concerns addressed?

627. How do you manage communications?

628. How were corresponding initiatives successful?

629. What is Management Staff Plan project communications management?

630. What help do you and your team need from the stakeholder?

631. What is the stakeholders level of authority?

632. Why do you manage communications?

633. Who will use or be affected by the result of a Management Staff Plan project?

634. Who to learn from?

2.31 Risk Management Plan: Management Staff Plan

635. Are staff committed for the duration of the product?

636. Minimize cost and financial risk?

637. Do you train all developers in the process?

638. Does the Management Staff Plan project have the authority and ability to avoid the risk?

639. Risk probability and impact: how will the probabilities and impacts of risk items be assessed?

640. Which is an input to the risk management process?

641. Have top software and customer managers formally committed to support the Management Staff Plan project?

642. Is there anything you would now do differently on your Management Staff Plan project based on this experience?

643. Who has experience with this?

644. Is the process being followed?

645. Does the customer have a solid idea of what is required?

646. Do you have a consistent repeatable process that is actually used?

647. Can the Management Staff Plan project proceed without assuming the risk?

648. Was an original risk assessment/risk management plan completed?

649. What is the impact to the Management Staff Plan project if the item is not resolved in a timely fashion?

650. Are team members trained in the use of the tools?

651. My Management Staff Plan project leader has suddenly left your organization, what do you do?

652. What are the chances the event will occur?

653. How is the audit profession changing?

654. Premium on reliability of product?

2.32 Risk Register: Management Staff Plan

655. Are your objectives at risk?

656. Technology risk -is the Management Staff Plan project technically feasible?

657. Who is going to do it?

658. Risk documentation: what reporting formats and processes will be used for risk management activities?

659. Budget and schedule: what are the estimated costs and schedules for performing risk-related activities?

660. Contingency actions - planned actions to reduce the immediate seriousness of the risk when it does occur. What should you do when?

661. Which key risks have ineffective responses or outstanding improvement actions?

662. When is it going to be done?

663. What is the appropriate level of risk management for this Management Staff Plan project?

664. What is the probability and impact of the risk occurring?

665. Methodology: how will risk management be

performed on this Management Staff Plan project?

666. People risk -are people with appropriate skills available to help complete the Management Staff Plan project?

667. What are you going to do to limit the Management Staff Plan projects risk exposure due to the identified risks?

668. Risk categories: what are the main categories of risks that should be addressed on this Management Staff Plan project?

669. What would the impact to the Management Staff Plan project objectives be should the risk arise?

670. Are there other alternative controls that could be implemented?

671. Who needs to know about this?

672. Severity Prediction?

673. Financial risk -can your organization afford to undertake the Management Staff Plan project?

2.33 Probability and Impact Assessment: Management Staff Plan

674. What will be cost of redeployment of personnel?

675. Sensitivity analysis -which risks will have the most impact on the Management Staff Plan project?

676. How much risk do others need to take?

677. Does the software interface with new or unproven hardware or unproven vendor products?

678. Has something like this been done before?

679. What are the current or emerging trends of culture?

680. Is the Management Staff Plan project cutting across the entire organization?

681. Assumptions analysis -what assumptions have you made or been given about your Management Staff Plan project?

682. Who should be responsible for the monitoring and tracking of the indicators youhave identified?

683. Are Management Staff Plan project requirements stable?

684. How do risks change during the Management Staff Plan projects life cycle?

685. Are the risk data complete?

686. Has the need for the Management Staff Plan project been properly established?

687. Why has this particular mode of contracting been chosen?

688. How do the products attain the specifications?

689. What can you do to minimize the impact if it does?

690. Your customers business requirements have suddenly shifted because of a new regulatory statute, what now?

691. Is the customer willing to establish rapid communication links with the developer?

2.34 Probability and Impact Matrix: Management Staff Plan

692. What are the channels available for distribution to the customer?

693. The customer requests a change to the Management Staff Plan project that would increase the Management Staff Plan project risk. Which should you do before ass the others?

694. Has the need for the Management Staff Plan project been properly established?

695. What should you do FIRST?

696. Can you avoid altogether some things that might go wrong?

697. Are enough people available?

698. Degree of confidence in estimated size estimate?

699. Prioritized components/features?

700. Who should be notified of the occurrence of each of the risk indicators?

701. Were there any Management Staff Plan projects similar to this one in existence?

702. What are data sources?

703. Are staff committed for the duration of the Management Staff Plan project?

704. What is the likelihood?

705. Is the delay in one subManagement Staff Plan project going to affect another?

706. How can you understand and diagnose risks and identify sources?

707. What are the ways you measure and evaluate risks?

708. Are you on schedule?

709. What are ways to measure and evaluate risks?

710. Who is going to be the consortium leader?

2.35 Risk Data Sheet: Management Staff Plan

711. Whom do you serve (customers)?

712. Risk of what?

713. How can it happen?

714. What if client refuses?

715. What are you trying to achieve (Objectives)?

716. What are your core values?

717. What is the chance that it will happen?

718. What will be the consequences if it happens?

719. What can you do?

720. Are new hazards created?

721. What are you here for (Mission)?

722. What are you weak at and therefore need to do better?

723. What actions can be taken to eliminate or remove risk?

724. What can happen?

725. How reliable is the data source?

726. Potential for recurrence?

727. What do you know?

728. What will be the consequences if the risk happens?

729. Who has a vested interest in how you perform as your organization (our stakeholders)?

2.36 Procurement Management Plan: Management Staff Plan

730. Are all resource assumptions documented?

731. Is Management Staff Plan project status reviewed with the steering and executive teams at appropriate intervals?

732. Does the schedule include Management Staff Plan project management time and change request analysis time?

733. Do all stakeholders know how to access the PM repository and where to find the Management Staff Plan project documentation?

734. Specific - is the objective clear in terms of what, how, when, and where the situation will be changed?

735. Are software metrics formally captured, analyzed and used as a basis for other Management Staff Plan project estimates?

736. Are key risk mitigation strategies added to the Management Staff Plan project schedule?

737. Is there a requirements change management processes in place?

738. Are meeting objectives identified for each meeting?

739. Are tasks tracked by hours?

740. Are risk triggers captured?

741. Have the key elements of a coherent Management Staff Plan project management strategy been established?

742. Do you have the reasons why the changes to your organizational systems and capabilities are required?

743. Does the Management Staff Plan project have a Statement of Work?

744. Have the key functions and capabilities been defined and assigned to each release or iteration?

745. Is Management Staff Plan project work proceeding in accordance with the original Management Staff Plan project schedule?

2.37 Source Selection Criteria: Management Staff Plan

746. What are the limitations on pre-competitive range communications?

747. What can not be disclosed?

748. Are resultant proposal revisions allowed?

749. Team leads: what is your process for assigning ratings?

750. What information may not be provided?

751. Do you want to have them collaborate at subfactor level?

752. What is the last item a Management Staff Plan project manager must do to finalize Management Staff Plan project close-out?

753. How should oral presentations be prepared for?

754. What documentation is needed for a tradeoff decision?

755. What risks were identified in the proposals?

756. What instructions should be provided regarding oral presentations?

757. Do you consider all weaknesses, significant

weaknesses, and deficiencies?

758. What are the special considerations for preaward debriefings?

759. Is a cost realism analysis used?

760. What should be the contracting officers strategy?

761. What is the role of counsel in the procurement process?

762. Is experience evaluated?

763. What information is to be provided and when should it be provided?

764. How do you manage procurement?

2.38 Stakeholder Management Plan: Management Staff Plan

765. Pareto diagrams, statistical sampling, flow charting or trend analysis used quality monitoring?

766. Have Management Staff Plan project management standards and procedures been identified / established and documented?

767. Is an industry recognized mechanized support tool(s) being used for Management Staff Plan project scheduling & tracking?

768. Who will the report(s) be delivered to?

769. Has a sponsor been identified?

770. What are reporting requirements?

771. Have reserves been created to address risks?

772. What records are required (eg purchase orders, agreements)?

773. Is the process working, and are people executing in compliance of the process?

774. Are you meeting your customers expectations consistently?

775. Has a Management Staff Plan project Communications Plan been developed?

776. Are the payment terms being followed?

777. Where will verification occur, and by whom?

778. Does the Management Staff Plan project have a formal Management Staff Plan project Plan?

779. Are Management Staff Plan project leaders committed to this Management Staff Plan project full time?

780. Are mitigation strategies identified?

2.39 Change Management Plan: Management Staff Plan

781. Identify the current level of skills and knowledge and behaviours of the group that will be impacted on. What prerequisite knowledge do corresponding groups need?

782. Who will be the change levers?

783. Who might be able to help you the most?

784. What are you trying to achieve as a result of communication?

785. What processes are in place to manage knowledge about the Management Staff Plan project?

786. Why is it important?

787. Clearly articulate the overall business benefits of the Management Staff Plan project -why are you doing this now?

788. Will the culture embrace or reject this change?

789. Do the proposed users have access to the appropriate documentation?

790. How far reaching in your organization is the change?

791. What are the key change management success

metrics?

792. What risks may occur upfront?

793. What are the essentials of the message?

794. Do you need new systems?

795. Different application of an existing process?

796. Has the training provider been established?

797. What is the reason for the communication?

3.0 Executing Process Group: Management Staff Plan

798. Does the Management Staff Plan project team have the right skills?

799. Do schedule issues conflicts?

800. Why should Management Staff Plan project managers strive to make jobs look easy?

801. Are escalated issues resolved promptly?

802. How do you enter durations, link tasks, and view critical path information?

803. Is the Management Staff Plan project performing better or worse than planned?

804. Who will be the main sponsor?

805. What are the main types of contracts if you do decide to outsource?

806. How does the job market and current state of the economy affect human resource management?

807. How do you measure difficulty?

808. Why do you need a good WBS to use Management Staff Plan project management software?

809. What is in place for ensuring adequate change control on Management Staff Plan projects that involve outside contracts?

810. Is activity definition the first process involved in Management Staff Plan project time management?

811. Are decisions made in a timely manner?

812. How well did the team follow the chosen processes?

813. What is the critical path for this Management Staff Plan project and how long is it?

814. Does the Management Staff Plan project team have enough people to execute the Management Staff Plan project plan?

815. Do your results resemble a normal distribution?

816. How does a Management Staff Plan project life cycle differ from a product life cycle?

3.1 Team Member Status Report: Management Staff Plan

817. How will resource planning be done?

818. Does your organization have the means (staff, money, contract, etc.) to produce or to acquire the product, good, or service?

819. Is there evidence that staff is taking a more professional approach toward management of your organizations Management Staff Plan projects?

820. Are the attitudes of staff regarding Management Staff Plan project work improving?

821. Are the products of your organizations Management Staff Plan projects meeting customers objectives?

822. Will the staff do training or is that done by a third party?

823. What is to be done?

824. Does the product, good, or service already exist within your organization?

825. Why is it to be done?

826. What specific interest groups do you have in place?

827. When a teams productivity and success depend on collaboration and the efficient flow of information, what generally fails them?

828. Are your organizations Management Staff Plan projects more successful over time?

829. Does every department have to have a Management Staff Plan project Manager on staff?

830. How does this product, good, or service meet the needs of the Management Staff Plan project and your organization as a whole?

831. The problem with Reward & Recognition Programs is that the truly deserving people all too often get left out. How can you make it practical?

832. Do you have an Enterprise Management Staff Plan project Management Office (EPMO)?

833. How can you make it practical?

834. How much risk is involved?

835. How it is to be done?

3.2 Change Request: Management Staff Plan

836. What are the duties of the change control team?

837. Who can suggest changes?

838. How can you ensure that changes have been made properly?

839. How shall the implementation of changes be recorded?

840. What is the change request log?

841. What kind of information about the change request needs to be captured?

842. How are changes graded and who is responsible for the rating?

843. Who needs to approve change requests?

844. Who will perform the change?

845. Will there be a change request form in use?

846. Will the change use memory to the extent that other functions will be not have sufficient memory to operate effectively?

847. Who is responsible for the implementation and monitoring of all measures?

848. How many lines of code must be changed to implement the change?

849. What should be regulated in a change control operating instruction?

850. How are changes requested (forms, method of communication)?

851. Has a formal technical review been conducted to assess technical correctness?

852. What has an inspector to inspect and to check?

853. Have all related configuration items been properly updated?

854. What are the requirements for urgent changes?

3.3 Change Log: Management Staff Plan

855. When was the request submitted?

856. How does this change affect scope?

857. Does the suggested change request seem to represent a necessary enhancement to the product?

858. Is this a mandatory replacement?

859. How does this relate to the standards developed for specific business processes?

860. Is the change request within Management Staff Plan project scope?

861. Where do changes come from?

862. Will the Management Staff Plan project fail if the change request is not executed?

863. Is the submitted change a new change or a modification of a previously approved change?

864. Do the described changes impact on the integrity or security of the system?

865. Who initiated the change request?

866. Is the requested change request a result of changes in other Management Staff Plan project(s)?

867. When was the request approved?

868. How does this change affect the timeline of the schedule?

869. Is the change backward compatible without limitations?

870. Is the change request open, closed or pending?

3.4 Decision Log: Management Staff Plan

871. How consolidated and comprehensive a story can you tell by capturing currently available incident data in a central location and through a log of key decisions during an incident?

872. Is your opponent open to a non-traditional workflow, or will it likely challenge anything you do?

873. What makes you different or better than others companies selling the same thing?

874. What was the rationale for the decision?

875. Linked to original objective?

876. Who will be given a copy of this document and where will it be kept?

877. Do strategies and tactics aimed at less than full control reduce the costs of management or simply shift the cost burden?

878. What eDiscovery problem or issue did your organization set out to fix or make better?

879. How does the use a Decision Support System influence the strategies/tactics or costs?

880. With whom was the decision shared or considered?

881. What alternatives/risks were considered?

882. Meeting purpose; why does this team meet?

883. Decision-making process; how will the team make decisions?

884. How do you know when you are achieving it?

885. What is the average size of your matters in an applicable measurement?

886. What are the cost implications?

887. What is the line where eDiscovery ends and document review begins?

888. It becomes critical to track and periodically revisit both operational effectiveness; Are you noticing all that you need to, and are you interpreting what you see effectively?

889. At what point in time does loss become unacceptable?

890. Adversarial environment. is your opponent open to a non-traditional workflow, or will it likely challenge anything you do?

3.5 Quality Audit: Management Staff Plan

891. How does your organization know that its information technology system is serving its needs as effectively and constructively as is appropriate?

892. How does your organization know that it is effectively and constructively guiding staff through to timely completion of tasks?

893. Has a written procedure been established to identify devices during all stages of receipt, reconditioning, distribution and installation so that mix-ups are prevented?

894. Do the acceptance procedures and specifications include the criteria for acceptance/rejection, define the process to be used, and specify the measuring and test equipment that is to be used?

895. Have personnel cleanliness and health requirements been established?

896. How does your organization know that its system for recruiting the best staff possible are appropriately effective and constructive?

897. How does your organization know that its security arrangements are appropriately effective and constructive?

898. Are training programs documented?

899. What are your supplier audits?

900. Are there sufficient personnel having the necessary education, background, training, and experience to assure that all operations are correctly performed?

901. Is there a written procedure for receiving materials?

902. Is quality audit a prerequisite for program accreditation or program recognition?

903. Are all employees including salespersons made aware that they must report all complaints received from any source for inclusion in the complaint handling system?

904. How does your organization know that its system for ensuring that its training activities are appropriately resourced and support is appropriately effective and constructive?

905. How do you indicate the extent to which your personnel would be expected to contribute to the work effort?

906. Are all employees made aware of device defects which may occur from the improper performance of specific jobs?

907. How does your organization know that its system for examining work done is appropriately effective and constructive?

908. How does your organization know whether they are adhering to mission and achieving objectives?

909. What does an analysis of your organizations staff profile suggest in terms of its planning, and how is this being addressed?

910. What has changed/improved as a result of the review processes?

3.6 Team Directory: Management Staff Plan

911. What are you going to deliver or accomplish?

912. Where should the information be distributed?

913. Process decisions: are contractors adequately prosecuting the work?

914. Who are the Team Members?

915. Do purchase specifications and configurations match requirements?

916. Process decisions: which organizational elements and which individuals will be assigned management functions?

917. Process decisions: do invoice amounts match accepted work in place?

918. Decisions: is the most suitable form of contract being used?

919. Days from the time the issue is identified?

920. How does the team resolve conflicts and ensure tasks are completed?

921. When will you produce deliverables?

922. Who will write the meeting minutes and

distribute?

923. Who is the Sponsor?

924. Who will talk to the customer?

925. Who are your stakeholders (customers, sponsors, end users, team members)?

926. Have you decided when to celebrate the Management Staff Plan projects completion date?

927. Decisions: what could be done better to improve the quality of the constructed product?

928. Process decisions: do job conditions warrant additional actions to collect job information and document on-site activity?

929. Process decisions: are all start-up, turn over and close out requirements of the contract satisfied?

3.7 Team Operating Agreement: Management Staff Plan

930. Are there more than two functional areas represented by your team?

931. Has the appropriate access to relevant data and analysis capability been granted?

932. How does teaming fit in with overall organizational goals and meet organizational needs?

933. Why does your organization want to participate in teaming?

934. Must your team members rely on the expertise of other members to complete tasks?

935. What administrative supports will be put in place to support the team and the teams supervisor?

936. Are there the right people on your team?

937. Do you brief absent members after they view meeting notes or listen to a recording?

938. Do you solicit member feedback about meetings and what would make them better?

939. What is a Virtual Team?

940. Communication protocols: how will the team communicate?

941. Did you delegate tasks such as taking meeting minutes, presenting a topic and soliciting input?

942. Have you established procedures that team members can follow to work effectively together, such as a team operating agreement?

943. How will group handle unplanned absences?

944. Conflict resolution: how will disputes and other conflicts be mediated or resolved?

945. Do you use a parking lot for any items that are important and outside of the agenda?

946. How do you want to be thought of and known within your organization?

947. The method to be used in the decision making process; Will it be consensus, majority rule, or the supervisor having the final say?

948. What are the current caseload numbers in the unit?

3.8 Team Performance Assessment: Management Staff Plan

949. Do friends perform better than acquaintances?

950. To what degree are the relative importance and priority of the goals clear to all team members?

951. What are teams?

952. When a reviewer complains about method variance, what is the essence of the complaint?

953. To what degree can team members vigorously define the teams purpose in considerations with others who are not part of the functioning team?

954. To what degree do team members frequently explore the teams purpose and its implications?

955. Do you promptly inform members about major developments that may affect them?

956. Individual task proficiency and team process behavior: what is important for team functioning?

957. Delaying market entry: how long is too long?

958. What makes opportunities more or less obvious?

959. To what degree can all members engage in open and interactive considerations?

960. To what degree are the teams goals and objectives clear, simple, and measurable?

961. Effects of crew composition on crew performance: Does the whole equal the sum of its parts?

962. To what degree do team members feel that the purpose of the team is important, if not exciting?

963. To what degree are corresponding categories of skills either actually or potentially represented across the membership?

964. To what degree are the skill areas critical to team performance present?

965. If you have received criticism from reviewers that your work suffered from method variance, what was the circumstance?

966. Can familiarity breed backup?

967. What are you doing specifically to develop the leaders around you?

968. To what degree is the team cognizant of small wins to be celebrated along the way?

3.9 Team Member Performance Assessment: Management Staff Plan

969. Why do performance reviews?

970. Is it clear how goals will be accomplished?

971. What qualities does a successful Team leader possess?

972. Which training platform formats (i.e., mobile, virtual, videogame-based) were implemented in your effort(s)?

973. How accurately is your plan implemented?

974. What makes them effective?

975. What does collaboration look like?

976. To what degree do team members articulate the teams work approach?

977. Are the draft goals SMART ?

978. How are evaluation results utilized?

979. What are the staffs preferences for training on technology-based platforms?

980. What are the basic principles and objectives of performance measurement and assessment?

981. How do you currently use the time that is available?

982. How do you know that all team members are learning?

983. To what extent did the evaluation influence the instructional path, such as with adaptive testing?

984. Where can team members go for more detailed information on performance measurement and assessment?

985. In what areas would you like to concentrate your knowledge and resources?

986. Are any validation activities performed?

987. How is the timing of assessments organized (e.g., pre/post-test, single point during training, multiple reassessment during training)?

988. To what degree does the teams purpose contain themes that are particularly meaningful and memorable?

3.10 Issue Log: Management Staff Plan

989. Where do team members get information?

990. What would have to change?

991. Are stakeholder roles recognized by your organization?

992. Do you feel a register helps?

993. Who is involved as you identify stakeholders?

994. What effort will a change need?

995. Do you feel more overwhelmed by stakeholders?

996. What is the impact on the Business Case?

997. Who is the issue assigned to?

998. Is there an important stakeholder who is actively opposed and will not receive messages?

999. How much time does it take to do it?

1000. Which stakeholders can influence others?

1001. Who are the members of the governing body?

1002. What approaches to you feel are the best ones to use?

1003. In classifying stakeholders, which approach to do so are you using?

1004. What is a Stakeholder?

1005. How do you manage human resources?

4.0 Monitoring and Controlling Process Group: Management Staff Plan

1006. What factors are contributing to progress or delay in the achievement of products and results?

1007. How well did the chosen processes fit the needs of the Management Staff Plan project?

1008. Overall, how does the program function to serve the clients?

1009. How were collaborations developed, and how are they sustained?

1010. Is there sufficient funding available for this?

1011. How is agile Management Staff Plan project management done?

1012. Feasibility: how much money, time, and effort can you put into this?

1013. Who are the Management Staff Plan project stakeholders?

1014. What resources are necessary?

1015. What do they need to know about the Management Staff Plan project?

1016. Were escalated issues resolved promptly?

1017. Are there areas that need improvement?

1018. How is agile program management done?

1019. What is the expected monetary value of the Management Staff Plan project?

1020. Is there undesirable impact on staff or resources?

1021. Did the Management Staff Plan project team have enough people to execute the Management Staff Plan project plan?

1022. What resources (both financial and non-financial) are available/needed?

4.1 Project Performance Report: Management Staff Plan

1023. To what degree are sub-teams possible or necessary?

1024. To what degree will the team ensure that all members equitably share the work essential to the success of the team?

1025. To what degree does the teams work approach provide opportunity for members to engage in fact-based problem solving?

1026. To what degree are the demands of the task compatible with and converge with the mission and functions of the formal organization?

1027. To what degree are the members clear on what they are individually responsible for and what they are jointly responsible for?

1028. To what degree is there a sense that only the team can succeed?

1029. To what degree does the team possess adequate membership to achieve its ends?

1030. To what degree does the funding match the requirement?

1031. What degree are the relative importance and priority of the goals clear to all team members?

1032. To what degree are the demands of the task compatible with and converge with the relationships of the informal organization?

1033. To what degree does the teams work approach provide opportunity for members to engage in results-based evaluation?

1034. To what degree do the structures of the formal organization motivate taskrelevant behavior and facilitate task completion?

1035. To what degree are the goals realistic?

1036. What is the degree to which rules govern information exchange between individuals within your organization?

1037. To what degree is there centralized control of information sharing?

1038. How will procurement be coordinated with other Management Staff Plan project aspects, such as scheduling and performance reporting?

1039. To what degree do team members understand one anothers roles and skills?

1040. To what degree can the cognitive capacity of individuals accommodate the flow of information?

4.2 Variance Analysis: Management Staff Plan

1041. Are your organizations and items of cost assigned to each pool identified?

1042. Do work packages consist of discrete tasks which are adequately described?

1043. How does your organization allocate the cost of shared expenses and services?

1044. Is work progressively subdivided into detailed work packages as requirements are defined?

1045. Are management actions taken to reduce indirect costs when there are significant adverse variances?

1046. Is data disseminated to the contractors management timely, accurate, and usable?

1047. What causes selling price variance?

1048. Who is generally responsible for monitoring and taking action on variances?

1049. Favorable or unfavorable variance?

1050. Are all budgets assigned to control accounts?

1051. How do you verify authorization to proceed with all authorized work?

1052. How are material, labor, and overhead variances calculated and recorded?

1053. How are variances affected by multiple material and labor categories?

1054. What is the expected future profitability of each customer?

1055. How does the use of a single conversion element (rather than the traditional labor and overhead elements) affect standard costing?

1056. Are overhead cost budgets established for each department which has authority to incur overhead costs?

1057. What is the actual cost of work performed?

4.3 Earned Value Status: Management Staff Plan

1058. Earned value can be used in almost any Management Staff Plan project situation and in almost any Management Staff Plan project environment. it may be used on large Management Staff Plan projects, medium sized Management Staff Plan projects, tiny Management Staff Plan projects (in cut-down form), complex and simple Management Staff Plan projects and in any market sector. some people, of course, know all about earned value, they have used it for years - but perhaps not as effectively as they could have?

1059. How much is it going to cost by the finish?

1060. What is the unit of forecast value?

1061. When is it going to finish?

1062. Verification is a process of ensuring that the developed system satisfies the stakeholders agreements and specifications; Are you building the product right? What do you verify?

1063. Are you hitting your Management Staff Plan projects targets?

1064. Where are your problem areas?

1065. If earned value management (EVM) is so good in determining the true status of a Management Staff

Plan project and Management Staff Plan project its completion, why is it that hardly any one uses it in information systems related Management Staff Plan projects?

1066. How does this compare with other Management Staff Plan projects?

1067. Validation is a process of ensuring that the developed system will actually achieve the stakeholders desired outcomes; Are you building the right product? What do you validate?

1068. Where is evidence-based earned value in your organization reported?

4.4 Risk Audit: Management Staff Plan

1069. Do staff understand the extent of duty of care?

1070. Do all coaches/instructors/leaders have appropriate and current accreditation?

1071. Do you have a realistic budget and do you present regular financial reports that identify how you are going against that budget?

1072. Is the auditor truly independent?

1073. The halo effect in business risk audits: can strategic risk assessment bias auditor judgment about accounting details?

1074. Are you aware of the industry standards that apply to your operations?

1075. What are the costs associated with late delivery or a defective product?

1076. Are procedures in place to ensure the security of staff and information and compliance with privacy legislation if applicable?

1077. What risk does not having unique identification present?

1078. Do you have a clear plan for the future that describes what you want to do and how you are going to do it?

1079. What are the commonly used work arounds in high risk areas?

1080. How effective are your risk controls?

1081. Does your board meet regularly and document all decisions and actions?

1082. Are policies communicated to all affected?

1083. Are audit program plans risk-adjusted?

1084. Do your financial policies and procedures ensure that each step in financial handling (receipt, recording, banking, reporting) is not completed by one person?

1085. Are risk management strategies documented?

1086. How do you govern assets?

1087. What does internal control mean in the context of the audit process?

1088. Have you considered the health and safety of everyone in your organization and do you meet work health and safety regulations?

4.5 Contractor Status Report: Management Staff Plan

1089. What was the final actual cost?

1090. What process manages the contracts?

1091. What is the average response time for answering a support call?

1092. What are the minimum and optimal bandwidth requirements for the proposed solution?

1093. Are there contractual transfer concerns?

1094. What was the budget or estimated cost for your organizations services?

1095. How is risk transferred?

1096. How long have you been using the services?

1097. What was the overall budget or estimated cost?

1098. If applicable; describe your standard schedule for new software version releases. Are new software version releases included in the standard maintenance plan?

1099. How does the proposed individual meet each requirement?

1100. Describe how often regular updates are made

to the proposed solution. Are corresponding regular updates included in the standard maintenance plan?

1101. Who can list a Management Staff Plan project as organization experience, your organization or a previous employee of your organization?

1102. What was the actual budget or estimated cost for your organizations services?

4.6 Formal Acceptance: Management Staff Plan

1103. How does your team plan to obtain formal acceptance on your Management Staff Plan project?

1104. Do you perform formal acceptance or burn-in tests?

1105. Was the sponsor/customer satisfied?

1106. Was the Management Staff Plan project work done on time, within budget, and according to specification?

1107. What lessons were learned about your Management Staff Plan project management methodology?

1108. Does it do what client said it would?

1109. Is formal acceptance of the Management Staff Plan project product documented and distributed?

1110. Was the Management Staff Plan project managed well?

1111. What is the Acceptance Management Process?

1112. What function(s) does it fill or meet?

1113. Was the Management Staff Plan project goal achieved?

1114. How well did the team follow the methodology?

1115. Does it do what Management Staff Plan project team said it would?

1116. Do you buy-in installation services?

1117. Who would use it?

1118. What was done right?

1119. Do you buy pre-configured systems or build your own configuration?

1120. What can you do better next time?

1121. What features, practices, and processes proved to be strengths or weaknesses?

1122. Who supplies data?

5.0 Closing Process Group: Management Staff Plan

1123. How will you know you did it?

1124. How well defined and documented were the Management Staff Plan project management processes you chose to use?

1125. Is this an updated Management Staff Plan project Proposal Document?

1126. How will staff learn how to use the deliverables?

1127. How critical is the Management Staff Plan project success to the success of your organization?

1128. What do you need to do?

1129. Is this a follow-on to a previous Management Staff Plan project?

1130. Is there a clear cause and effect between the activity and the lesson learned?

1131. What areas were overlooked on this Management Staff Plan project?

1132. Did the Management Staff Plan project team have the right skills?

1133. What is the overall risk of the Management Staff Plan project to your organization?

1134. What areas does the group agree are the biggest success on the Management Staff Plan project?

1135. Were cost budgets met?

1136. What is the amount of funding and what Management Staff Plan project phases are funded?

1137. Did you do things well?

1138. Is the Management Staff Plan project funded?

5.1 Procurement Audit: Management Staff Plan

1139. Did your organization state the minimum requirements to be met by the variants in the tender documents?

1140. Is there no evidence of any individual on the evaluation panel being biased?

1141. Are travel expenditures monitored to determine that they are in line with other employees and reasonable for the area of travel?

1142. Is there a practice that prohibits signing blank purchase orders?

1143. Are there procedures for trade-in arrangements?

1144. Was the estimation of contract value in accordance with the criteria fixed in the Directive?

1145. Have late payment interests been rewarded and could they have been avoided?

1146. Are buyers prohibited from accepting gifts from vendors?

1147. Is there a purchasing policy as to the amount of an order on which bidding is required?

1148. Are all mutilated and voided checks retained for

proper accounting of pre-numbered checks?

1149. Was the payment made to the supplier/ contractor within the time frames indicated in the contracts?

1150. Does your organization make sources of information beyond the tender documents equally available for all the candidates?

1151. Was the suitability of candidates accurately assessed?

1152. Are bank accounts reconciled by an individual independent of the disbursement responsibilities?

1153. Are the official minutes written in a clear and concise manner?

1154. Are eu procurement regulations applicable?

1155. Are controls proportionated to risks?

1156. Are procedures established on how orders will be shipped?

1157. Are approval limits covered in written procedures?

1158. Which are main risks and controls of each phase?

5.2 Contract Close-Out: Management Staff Plan

1159. Change in attitude or behavior?

1160. Was the contract sufficiently clear so as not to result in numerous disputes and misunderstandings?

1161. Was the contract type appropriate?

1162. Change in knowledge?

1163. Parties: who is involved?

1164. Have all contract records been included in the Management Staff Plan project archives?

1165. Have all contracts been closed?

1166. Change in circumstances?

1167. Have all contracts been completed?

1168. Have all acceptance criteria been met prior to final payment to contractors?

1169. Are the signers the authorized officials?

1170. Why Outsource?

1171. What is capture management?

1172. How is the contracting office notified of the

automatic contract close-out?

1173. Was the contract complete without requiring numerous changes and revisions?

1174. How does it work?

1175. Has each contract been audited to verify acceptance and delivery?

1176. Parties: Authorized?

1177. What happens to the recipient of services?

1178. How/when used ?

5.3 Project or Phase Close-Out: Management Staff Plan

1179. Which changes might a stakeholder be required to make as a result of the Management Staff Plan project?

1180. What were the actual outcomes?

1181. What is a Risk?

1182. What hierarchical authority does the stakeholder have in your organization?

1183. What are the marketing communication needs for each stakeholder?

1184. What could be done to improve the process?

1185. What could have been improved?

1186. Were messages directly related to the release strategy or phases of the Management Staff Plan project?

1187. What were the desired outcomes?

1188. Did the Management Staff Plan project management methodology work?

1189. What were the goals and objectives of the communications strategy for the Management Staff Plan project?

1190. What information is each stakeholder group interested in?

1191. How often did each stakeholder need an update?

1192. When and how were information needs best met?

1193. What advantages do the an individual interview have over a group meeting, and vice-versa?

1194. Does the lesson educate others to improve performance?

1195. In addition to assessing whether the Management Staff Plan project was successful, it is equally critical to analyze why it was or was not fully successful. Are you including this?

1196. What is a Risk Management Process?

1197. Planned remaining costs?

5.4 Lessons Learned: Management Staff Plan

1198. How well does the product or service the Management Staff Plan project produced meet the defined Management Staff Plan project requirements?

1199. What is the distribution of authority?

1200. How to write up the lesson identified – how will you document the results of your analysis corresponding that you have an li ready to take the next step in the ll process?

1201. What is the growth stage of the organization?

1202. Who had fiscal authority to manage the funding for the Management Staff Plan project, did that work?

1203. What is the fiscal dependency?

1204. How effective was Management Staff Plan project Team member training?

1205. How well prepared were you to receive Management Staff Plan project deliverables?

1206. How effective was each Management Staff Plan project Team member in fulfilling his/her role?

1207. Were any objectives unmet?

1208. How complete and timely were the materials

you were provided to decide whether to proceed from one Management Staff Plan project lifecycle phase to the next?

1209. Is the lesson based on actual Management Staff Plan project experience rather than on independent research?

1210. Whom to share Lessons Learned Information with?

1211. Was the purpose of the Management Staff Plan project, the end products and success criteria clearly defined and agreed at the start?

1212. Why does your organization need a lessons learned (LL) capability?

1213. How much of your time was spent on other than this Management Staff Plan project?

1214. How effective were Management Staff Plan project audits?

1215. How actively and meaningfully were stakeholders involved in the Management Staff Plan project?

1216. How efficient is the deliverable?

1217. What were the success factors?

Index

278

292

prevented   228
prevents   18
previous   39, 164, 176, 252, 255
previously   224
primary   48
principles   138, 196, 237
printing   8
priorities   50-51, 54, 57-58
priority 46, 58, 163, 235, 243
privacy   34, 249
probably   170
problem   17-18, 20, 22-24, 26, 28, 34-35, 38, 40, 45, 52, 67,
73, 145, 221, 226, 243, 247
problems   19-20, 22, 25-26, 90-91, 101, 146, 150, 189-190
procedure   228-229
procedures   11, 95, 98, 101-102, 142-143, 152, 156, 168, 177,
188, 214, 228, 234, 249-250, 257-258
proceed   201, 245, 264
proceeding   174, 196, 211
process   1-7, 11, 28, 36, 39-40, 42, 58, 61-63, 65-66, 68-73,
75, 82, 90, 94, 96-104, 131, 138, 141, 144, 146, 148, 151-153, 158-
159, 168, 172, 174, 179, 185, 187, 190-191, 194, 200-201, 212-214,
217-219, 227-228, 231-232, 234-235, 241, 247-248, 250-251, 253,
255, 261-263
processes   53, 56, 63-67, 69-71, 74-75, 96, 103, 131, 158, 186-
187, 202, 210, 216, 219, 224, 230, 241, 254-255
produce   134, 168, 220, 231
produced   75, 263
producing   148
product   1, 11, 68-69, 115, 119, 139, 143-144, 151, 184, 189,
200-201, 219-221, 224, 232, 247-249, 253, 263
production   30, 82, 110, 137
products   1, 26, 52, 122, 134, 148, 156, 184, 204-205, 220,
241, 264
profession   201
profile 230
program   21, 56, 70, 95, 143, 187, 195, 229, 241-242, 250
programs   198, 221, 228
progress   29, 48, 90, 99, 109, 183, 190-191, 241
prohibited   157, 257
prohibits   257

project 2-4, 6-7, 9, 19-20, 25, 33, 55, 67, 74, 81, 98, 100, 103, 107-110, 112, 118, 124, 127-128, 130-144, 148, 150-155, 158, 160-161, 164, 166-167, 170-171, 173-186, 188, 192-197, 199-207, 210-212, 214-216, 218-221, 224, 241-244, 247-248, 252-256, 259, 261-264
projected   157, 184
projects   2, 51, 111, 123, 130, 133, 137-138, 148, 152, 155, 173, 176, 179, 184, 198, 203-204, 206, 219-221, 232, 247-248
promising   115
promote   52, 67
promptly   218, 235, 241
proofing   82
proper 104, 156, 179, 186, 258
properly   11, 37-38, 205-206, 222-223
proposal   164, 212, 255
proposals   95, 172, 212
proposed   19, 48-49, 216, 251-252
protect   69, 126
protected   75
protection   125
protocols   233
proved 254
provide   21, 114, 121, 135, 147, 156, 166, 174, 182, 192, 243-244
provided   8, 13, 93, 143, 212-213, 264
provider   217
providers   86
provides   147, 164
providing   104, 135
provision   197
public 137
publisher   1
pulled 123
purchase   9, 11, 214, 231, 257
purchased   11
purchasing   257
purpose   2, 11, 111, 134, 137, 171, 182, 227, 235-236, 238, 264
pushing   127
qualified   29, 62, 74, 76, 172
qualifies   65, 67
qualify 46, 62, 66
qualifying   176
qualities   25, 237

quality 1, 4-5, 11, 27, 46, 48, 51, 62, 68, 80, 103, 117, 136, 159, 172-173, 177-178, 186-191, 194-195, 197, 214, 228-229, 232
quantified   95
quantify   46
question   12-13, 17, 28, 45, 61, 77, 93, 106, 138, 191
questions   7, 9, 12, 67, 144, 150
quickly 12, 62, 70-71, 192
radically   63
raised 150
rather 59, 119, 246, 264
rating 222
ratings 212
rational   157
rationale   226
reached   26
reaching   112, 216
reactivate   115
readiness   31, 196
readings   101
realism 213
realistic   26, 64, 119, 172, 244, 249
realize 53
really   7, 24, 35, 193
reason 120, 126, 217
reasonable   91, 140, 153, 159, 197, 257
reasons   38, 211
reassess   197
re-assign   162
rebuild 115
recasts 180
receipt 228, 250
receive   9-10, 32, 58, 239, 263
received   29, 229, 236
receiving   229
recently   11, 108
recipient   18, 260
recognised   84
recognize   2, 17, 21, 24-25, 80, 82, 90
recognized   18, 20-23, 27, 72, 214, 239
recognizes   22
recommend   113, 120, 151
reconciled   258
recorded   222, 246

CPSIA information can be obtained
at www.ICGtesting.com
Printed in the USA
BVHW041757290719
554530BV00036B/936/P

9 780655 827252